MAD | HUNGRY

MAD HUNGRY

Feeding Men and Boys

RECIPES, STRATEGIES, AND SURVIVAL TECHNIQUES

Lucinda Scala Quinn

PHOTOGRAPHS
by Mikkel Vang

ARTISAN

dedication

To my mother, Rosemary Jean Scala,
for showing me how and why to cook
for those you love

Published by Artisan
A Division of Workman Publishing, Inc.
225 Varick Street
New York, NY 10014-4381
www.artisanbooks.com

Published simultaneously in Canada by Thomas Allen & Son, Limited

Library of Congress Cataloging-in-Publication Data
Scala Quinn, Lucinda.
Mad hungry: feeding men and boys / by Lucinda Scala Quinn.
p. cm.
ISBN 978-1-57965-356-9
1. Cookery. I. Title.
TX714.Q587 2009
641.5—dc22 2009004063

Design by Jennifer S. Muller, Lucky Tangerine

Printed in Singapore

7 9 10 8 6

contents

05 | Down-home Desserts $\qquad$ 221
They'll Take It Any Way They Can Get It

preface | my story

The secret rites of the kitchen need not be a mystery.
Slowly build your specialized cooking knowledge, day after day, as you
cook for the ones you love. Your table will be full, and one day the guys
will wander into the kitchen, too. In the beginning, they'll slip in to steal
a nibble before dinner, dipping some bread into the simmering tomato
sauce or picking the browned bits from the fried chicken. And eventually,
if they join you in these regions, the spirit will take hold.

I began to teach our firstborn, Calder, to cook when he was fifteen
years old as a trade-off for more allowance. Now he's the one
giving me recipes (see page 122).

Miles, our middle son, is a professional teenage cook, just like his
mother was. And the baby, Luca, for whom eating hearty food is a favorite
pastime (along with athletics, fortunately), is just learning to cook.

My husband, Richie, has a huge appetite for life—all of it—and food is at the
top of his list. Unlike me, he is a bit of a rogue as a cook (lots of spice and darkly
caramelized meats), but his passion in the kitchen is infectious and has
inspired me over the last twenty-five years as well as the boys.

My own influence comes from my parents. My mom, Rose, made
home-cooked meals for me and my brothers, day in and day out. And my
dad's Italian heritage meant my early years were filled with extended
family gatherings that always centered on a bounty of food.

All of our stories are different, yet still, there are new chapters to be written.

introduction
cook for the men in your life and teach them to cook for themselves

Men eat differently from women—they eat more, they eat constantly, and they eat passionately. They ransack a packed refrigerator and scrounge crumbs from an empty one. They eat standing in front of the fridge, and they eat with their fingers. They always make a mess and never notice. They are all appetite and no pretense. "What's for dinner?" is the most important, most burning question. Food is everything to them and food is nothing until there is none. And, if they're "mad hungry" with no food in sight, life is a living hell. But feeding them well is what many of us love to do and few jobs feel as satisfying. It's what keeps them healthy, keeps them happy, gives them some of their fondest memories, and teaches them to cook.

Boys and men who grow up eating flavorful home-cooked food are more likely to cook for themselves. A man who knows how to cook is more self-sufficient, is a better roommate, boyfriend, father, and son. And as any wife knows, a husband who can cook is like one who can dance—the deluxe package.

So no matter how busy you are, sauté that onion, rip up fresh basil, or slow-roast a pork shoulder. That's all it takes to fill their sense memory and make your family feel good for a lifetime. When I last gave a steaming bowl of lentil soup to one of my sons, his casual remark spoke volumes: "That smell right there—that's comfort food. It makes you feel happy." Once, another son arrived home from college, walked through the front door, and announced, unbidden, "It smells so good in here. Sometimes I think I cook to re-create the smells I'm nostalgic for from your cooking." Instead of being a chore, mealtime can be the foundation of a wonderful relationship with the men and boys in your life.

Feeding my four guys has been one of the greatest pleasures of my life. I've had more fun in the kitchen and at the dinner table with them than almost anywhere else. Eating is something we have to do, so why give it short shrift? If you have to do it, make it beautiful and spread the beauty.

Home cooking feels good, is healthier and cheaper, and tastes better than processed food. It also liberates you from the angst-ridden daily choices of food labels that scream low-fat, low-salt, high-carb, low-carb, artificially sweetened or, worse, promise better health (all-natural) when there is none. The whole fast-food approach is leading us down the wrong ugly path. Now is the time to do something about it. Cook good, honest food and the rest will take care of itself.

If you were never taught to cook or appreciate a home-cooked meal, all the more reason to give your taste buds and those of your family a gift. If there's a will, there's a way. Find help all around you, from a grandparent, family friend, favorite teacher, book, or cooking class. Go step by step, because no matter where you start, it's a trial by fire for all of us who cook for men. Whether you adapt the ideas in this book or gaze at them from a distance, like folks who watch cooking shows but don't cook, you've planted the seed for yourself and your guys. Create your own recipe collection, choose what you love, and cook it often; the common thread in this cookbook is nothing more than dishes my family loves.

Start off slow if you must. Cook just one meal a week and see for yourself what a difference it makes. Most of all be delighted with the time you and your men have together in the kitchen, whether cooking or sitting around the table eating homemade food. As your brood spreads out, these warm memories of good home cooking will guide them home and, having learned to cook themselves, they will pass it on.

"It seems to me that our three basic needs,
for food and security and love, are so mixed and
mingled and entwined that we cannot straightly think
of one without the others. So it happens that when I write
of hunger, I am really writing about love and the hunger
for it, and warmth and the love of it and the hunger
for it . . . and then the warmth and richness and fine
reality of hunger satisfied . . . and it is all one."

—M. F. K. Fisher from *The Gastronomical Me*, 1943

The ten tenets

an action plan for how and why to feed your guys

just do it.

You have to. It's your community. You're the president, the governor, the mayor, the boss, and the grown-up.

1
Decide it's important to you

When the household cooks have jobs outside the home and still want daily home-cooked meals, a conscious decision has to be made to place value on this practice. We need to commit to it and collaborate with each other to achieve success. It's no different from creating any other aspect of a balanced home life.

2
Educate yourself

You can begin cooking at any phase of life. It's better than never beginning at all. The resources to draw from are endless: cookbooks, culinary schools, television shows, and online tutorials are available for just about anything you might want to learn. If you've just started out cooking for a man or your family, make it simple and make it something you enjoy. Any great education is acquired over years; you don't one day suddenly say to yourself, "I think I'll purchase that wisdom now." It's the same with becoming a cook. Daily practice will lead you there, and each day will get easier and better.

3
Practice simple recipes

Men like simple, straightforward foods. Don't try to follow multiple new recipes at the same time. Focus on one, then round out the rest of the meal with basic standbys like baked potatoes, steamed vegetables, or a simple salad. It's difficult to follow too many cooking instructions simultaneously. Those of us who cook daily for our mate or family need energy and high productivity for this task, not frustration and exhaustion. When following any recipe, first read it through completely, then gather and prepare all the ingredients and tools before you start cooking and put each item away as it is used. Don't let a recipe eliminate your spontaneity, but remember any art or craft requires technique, which is acquired only through repetition.

4
Think strategy

With a family to feed, you have to avoid getting caught short at mealtime without a strategy and supplies in place. Disorganization is ultimately more time-consuming, stressful, and costly than forethought and planning. Set aside time to plan your meals. Try to shop weekly and learn to efficiently navigate your local markets. If your goal is to cook easily at home then food shopping is half the battle (see Food Shopping, page 6). Every night review your mental checklist for tomorrow's breakfast, lunch bag, and dinner.

Make one dinner, the same for every family member. Never fill the plates too full, and always have enough for seconds and thirds. Don't ask them if they're hungry—just put the food on the table. Don't wait for the boys to ask for or want breakfast, lunch, or dinner—just cook it and serve it because young boys don't always ask to eat until they're ravenous and cranky. Anticipate their needs before they melt down.

5
Economize resources

In just about every way, home cooking is better than purchasing less healthful and more costly meals outside the home. And, the most frugal survival technique for the daily feeding of hungry growing boys is the strategic planning of menus, marketing, and cooking. Instead of just thinking about making a "twenty-minute meal," think about reorganizing your day into blocks of time: Spend fifteen or twenty minutes organizing and prepping the previous night or in the morning before work. Tag-team with another household member after school or work to move the recipe along. Then take fifteen minutes to finish pulling the whole thing together just before dinner. With supplies in the house and a written plan taped on the refrigerator, you can stretch your time and your money.

And since economy also means conserving on resources, try letting appliances do double duty. If you turn the oven on for a roast chicken, why not oven-roast the vegetables at the same time? Two medium-sized chickens come to about twenty dollars. Add some rice and vegetables, and you can healthfully fill the stomachs of five boys for less than twenty-five dollars. Compare that to five not-so-happy, nutritionless Happy Meals at about five dollars each, along with the gas it takes to drive to the restaurant, and the family dinner choice is a no-brainer.

6
Be a mealtime evangelist

Eat breakfast yourself. Sit down to dinner. Model the behavior and walk it like you talk it. After years of cooking meals, and joining your family at the table, you'll be rewarded and thankful for what has taken place.

Create a legacy. Serve old-fashioned—meaning simple—meals, the kind moms everywhere have always made. When I was a kid, meals were predictable, comforting, familiar, tasty, and most of all consistent. Anyone who grew up with someone cooking regular meals remembers those dishes as if they were eaten yesterday. For me, it's leftover pork, stir-fried with vegetables and served over a pile of rice, a frequent meal I took for granted but now look back on with great nostalgia. I asked family and friends to recall their favorite family meals, and they all came up with an answer immediately: taco night, chicken and dumplings, pot roast served with potato pancakes and applesauce, red beans and rice.

If you missed out—in a home of fast food or where mealtime was a pain instead of a pleasure—you can break the mold now. Start your own traditions for feeding yourself, your men, your boys (and the girls and women who love them) at home.

7 Keep 'em healthy

Home-cooked dinners pretty much guarantee better ingredients—more fruits and vegetables, complex carbohydrates, and proteins—everything that turns healthy boys into healthy men. This is your chance to keep chemically processed foods high in sugar, salt, and fat out of their diets.

- Cook vegetables correctly, and you'll convert the most adamant anti-veg guy in your family. Offer a few choices on the plate for dinner every night from day one, each vegetable cooked using a simple technique—lightly steamed spinach (page 93), Braised Green Beans (page 214), and Carmelized Cauliflower (page 202). Your guys will definitely fall for (if not love) them, even though their hearts will still belong to fried chicken.

- Always prepare an abundance of **grains**. Extra rice, pasta, or couscous will stretch any meal, serve as second helpings, create a platform for the next morning's eggs, and add needed daily fiber for a body's well-being.

- Don't be afraid of **beans and legumes**. Black beans, red beans, chickpeas, or lentils can be the star of a meal, providing protein without the need for meat. Look to different cultures for recipes, especially ones that have sustained families for centuries, like Indian-style chickpeas, Latin-style black beans, and French lentils. Savory, robust spicing and condiments make these dishes truly delicious. And one meatless day a week will reduce your carbon footprint.

- Think of **meat** as a component of the meal rather than the star. Try different cuts, ones with bones, such as chuck steak—they offer more flavor and are often less expensive. A stew stretched with vegetables smothered in a meaty sauce can stand in for the beloved burger and steak dinner now and then.

8 Trade food for talk

If you make breakfast, lunch, and dinner every day, chances are at least one of these meals will be consumed as a family and a meal eaten together almost always engenders conversation. If you sit down to a home-cooked meal, take your husband or kids to the market with you, or ask for their help in the kitchen, you're establishing a common vocabulary. They might not want to talk, but they always want to eat, and they'll talk to you about that. This is doubly true for adolescent boys: they might be in their surliest years, but they're also in their hungriest. Food is a vehicle for conversation, but not necessarily the topic of it. Whatever tension might be in the air, a request such as "Pass the potatoes" opens a crack in the door to conversation, and before you know it, someone is relating something about his day, another pipes in, and then suddenly it's a no-holds-barred conversation. What better way is there to learn about the people you love?

9
Train them to fend for themselves

As the Chinese proverb almost says: "Cook a man some food and you feed him for a meal. Teach him to cook meals and you feed him for a lifetime." Inspire them to cook food themselves. Train your boys to become self-sufficient men when it comes to the kitchen. This is an essential life skill, like brushing your teeth, keeping yourself clean, or getting to work on time. When our oldest boy began cooking in high school, he thought it'd be a snap—but, after a few disasters (no, a "clove" of garlic isn't a "head" of garlic), we figured out he needed some serious schooling, so week after week, I walked him through:

Basic Skills and a Few of Our House Standards

- Work on a clean cutting board: to stabilize it, place a wet paper towel or thin cloth towel underneath.

- Cut an onion with a sharp knife (see page 3). To peel it, first slice it in half lengthwise. Place the cut sides down on the board. Cut off the root end of both halves and remove the skin. For slices, make thin vertical cuts side by side on each half. To chop, cut each half again horizontally, across the slices to create small pieces (try to keep the half-onion shape intact while cutting).

- Mince the garlic: Separate an individual clove from the large head, whack it with the side of a knife on the cutting board, and the skin will slide right off. Cut off the root end. Slice the clove and work the knife across the slices several times (keep wiping the garlic pieces off the knife), gather into a small pile, and repeat until you have very fine pieces.

- Simmer the tomato sauce (see page 179) and properly cook the pasta (two minutes short of package instructions).

- Roast two chickens (remove the cavity bag) side by side (head to toe, breast down first for even cooking) on a rack or a bed of thick-sliced onions or platform of stale bread in a roasting pan.

- Bake eight whole potatoes or sweet potatoes, unpeeled and washed (pierce with a fork or they explode), at the same time as the chickens roast, while a couple of heads of sectioned broccoli (including the stems cut into coins) steam on the stove top.

10
Cook most days with pleasure

Sure, preparing meals is sometimes a thankless job, one the family cook can barely stand at times. An especially unruly night is daunting. Cries of "I hate fish," or "The meat's undercooked," or "Broccoli again?" are discouraging. But, don't take it to heart. If you don't love to cook, you can at least take pleasure in the fact that you're doing something good for the people you love.

tools,
flavors,
and theories

You don't need that much to get started in the kitchen and enjoy the results of satisfying meals. Invest in a few quality essential items rather than overloading yourself with too many.

a few good knives

There's no getting around the necessity of a good, sharp knife for an everyday cook.

When I started cooking professionally as a sixteen-year-old, a knife was my first purchase. I did every task with a six-inch Sabatier carbon-steel knife that I cared for obsessively because it would rust with the slightest bit of water left clinging to it.

Nowadays, knife makers from different countries offer an array of styles, blades, and handles. Three types—chef's, paring, and serrated—will handle any task. But preferences vary from cook to cook—where one might prefer a large chef's knife, another might prefer a slicer, and still another gets everything done with a paring knife. You should buy knives that fit your hand and use them all the time. Don't let anyone tell you what "should" be used.

USING A KNIFE

- Grip the handle firmly with your thumb planted on the top side of the dull edge, just below where the blade meets the handle. Evenly curl your fingers around underneath the handle using your pinky to anchor the grip.

- Always chop on a cutting board.

- Hold whatever you are cutting with the fingertips of your opposite hand curled under (to avoid slicing a fingertip), using your knuckles as a guide for the side of the blade. Gently slice or chop from the tip backward.

SHARPENING A KNIFE

- Don't wait ten years to learn how to sharpen your knives. It's worthwhile knowledge and will make cooking so much more pleasurable and easier. If you've ever tried chopping onions with a dull knife you know what I mean.

- Keeping your knives sharp is a must! Sharpen each knife before extended use, wipe it down immediately after you're finished, and put it away.

- You'll need a sharpening stone and a honing steel. Sharpen your knife on the stone at least once a month, then hone by sliding the blade up and down on both sides of the honing steel. Follow the manufacturer's directions for usage. Hone your knife before each use. Practice will make these actions feel natural.

- Some honing steels come with a stone groove above the handle. I'm not a fan, but I'd rather use one than use a dull knife.

note

Beware of a son who takes to cooking professionally. Knives will become his first obsession. Keeping him outfitted in knives is no different than the constant expense of soccer cleats or hockey skates.

When your home is child-free, you can display your knives on a magnet under the cabinets or in a knife block. So far I've avoided leaving them out in plain view, a little too tempting for a bunch of boys—and men—to use for cutting up any manner of nonfood objects.

cast-iron pans

If I were forced to choose one favorite pan, cast iron would be it. It cooks and bakes and travels from stove top to oven to table. It gets very hot and retains heat. Properly seasoned, it's the best searing pan there is. And it adds valuable iron to your diet: with only ten milligrams required daily for men and women, it's easy to get a percentage of that in your food just through the cooking process.

NEW CAST IRON, LIKE A FRESH PAIR OF LEVI'S, NEEDS TO BE BROKEN IN

- Fill it with vegetable oil and place in a 200°F oven for 90 minutes.

- Drain and discard the oil, and wipe the pan clean.

- Coat the bottom of the pan in oil for its first few uses.

DON'T USE SOAP TO CLEAN CAST IRON

- To clean cast iron, simply wipe out the pan with a paper towel or a cloth. Soap eliminates the carefully acquired patina achieved over time, taking you right back to where you started.

- For a more stubborn mess, rinse in warm water and scrape with a firm metal spatula. Fully dry the pan by placing it on a burner over high heat, as if beginning to cook, for 30 seconds. The moisture will

evaporate and the pan will self-season as the heat releases some oil (use more oil if necessary). Wipe the pan down and put it away.

- If a soap crime is committed, just reseason and start over.

THREE PERFECT SIZES

- A 14-inch pan is a life-altering addition to the working-family kitchen because it will allow you to fry chicken in one batch!

- A 12-inch pan is perfect for frittatas or a couple of steaks.

- A 6-inch pan is ideal for fried eggs.

You can find new cast-iron pans for reasonable prices—hardware stores carry 12-inch skillets for twenty-five dollars—or you can buy used ones at flea markets; just clean and reseason them. Buy one and you'll be hooked for life. And one day, these pans might find their way to your son's new home.

Dutch oven

An enameled cast-iron Dutch oven is a crucial kitchen investment for the everyday cook. This is especially true if you're cooking for a brood and want to make large quantities of soups, stews, and other braises. Many of these dishes start with the browning or searing of meat, followed by steady and lengthy simmering, both of which are performed beautifully in this cooking vessel.

We have an enameled cast-iron Dutch oven that has been in the family for more than forty years. Made by Le Creuset in an orange-flame color, it has traveled from coast to coast and oven to oven. It sits above our stove in full view, along with a few others of various sizes; I like to see functional yet beautiful kitchenware out in the open, with all their well-worn scars and imperfections.

A Dutch oven can be used for a lifetime and passed on. To glimpse inside a well-used one is to imagine the many meals made and mouths fed. You might want to collect a few different sizes—a 4-quart Dutch oven makes an excellent rice pot, for example. Ovenproof, it easily moves from stove top to oven to table and it keeps food warm along the way since the heavy iron retains heat.

Food Shopping

As any parent or head of household knows, food shopping is a necessity, but many people don't realize the crucial role consistent shopping plays in your ability to cook every day. Treated as an afterthought rather than as a regular strategy, your cooking and eating life becomes a constant game of catch-up. Always stay a step ahead with a plan and you'll find that meals are easier to execute and your kitchen will run more smoothly.

Make a weekly plan for visiting your favorite or most convenient markets. Place a standing order with your local market or open an online account with a food vendor.

SHOPPING TIPS FOR NAVIGATING YOUR LOCAL MARKETS:

- Begin in the meat section. For my family of five, I might choose two chickens, a pork shoulder, and two pounds of cut-up stew beef as a starting point to build the week's evening meals. Three evenings of meat are interspersed with a bean night, a pasta night, and a soup night.

- Buy enough vegetables for three days; fresh produce is easy to supplement during the week. Keep a constant supply of onions and garlic. Always have frozen peas and corn on hand.

- Buy a half gallon each of milk, preferably organic—devoid of added hormones or antibiotics—and orange juice for the refrigerator, plus one or two of each to freeze. Butter freezes well, too. Thaw the liquids by placing the cartons in the sink for several hours or, for a shorter thaw, rest the cartons in a bowl of hot water. Thaw the butter by putting it in the fridge.

- Buy large bottles of unsweetened seltzer instead of soda and juice laced with high-fructose corn syrup. Read the ingredients. High-fructose corn syrup lurks in some very unlikely seeming products such as granola bars, yogurt, and crackers. Train your guys early on to enjoy filtered tap water and to drink lots of it. Convince them by telling them how important it is to avoid dehydration. It saps energy, makes you feel tired, and can lead to headaches and dizziness. Drinking plenty of water also cleanses toxins from the body and promotes healthy skin (boys with acne take note!).

- Buy and freeze fresh bread. If it's already sliced, pop the bag in the freezer and use slices as needed for sandwiches (a good method to lengthen the life of a lunch-box sandwich), or for toast. You can freeze a whole loaf in a bag or cut it into sections, wrap the pieces in foil, and bag, to be defrosted in large chunks as needed. If you buy multipacks of bread, then freezing fresh bread is essential since defrosted bread tastes much better than day-old bread.

- Return home from the grocery store and jot down your weekly menus while deciding what to freeze and what to use within the next few days. If you can, take some time to prepare a few items for that night's dinner and review your plan for breakfast and lunch the next day. Clean and store fresh greens (see page 89). That way they'll be ready at a moment's notice so you'll be much more likely to serve healthful salads (see page 89).

- Seek out the local markets when traveling. It's a great way to get a true sense of the place. Check out what items are on the grocer's shelves in that particular town or country and how they're used. The market is often a community center filled with a diverse cross section of people, politics, and possibilities.

shopping with the kids

Taking young children to the market with you can be
an inconvenience. Instead, turn food shopping
into a teaching opportunity.

- Let them sniff and hold items in the produce section. Identify fruits and vegetables and say, "This is what a real peach smells like. If it doesn't smell like a peach, it probably won't taste like one." Instruct them to pick up each zucchini or head of garlic and examine it. Teach them to look for bruises or soft spots or to tell if an item is dried out. Show them how to choose cherries—and how not to hurry. Let them know that one rotten piece of fruit will ruin the whole bunch if left together in a bag. Pick each one, one at a time.

- Divide your shopping list into sections under headings: meat, dairy, produce, breadstuff, and pantry. Give a short list to a child who is old enough to collect items himself and send him to the corresponding section in the store. If he picks up the wrong item, be patient and use it as a coachable moment. Next time give a better description—for example, "the one with the house on the package." He'll return proud of his accomplishment and you will have taught independence and communication skills.

- Find ways to excite your children's interest in shopping. One market in New York City provides jackets that customers can don before they enter the cold room where the meats are stored. My mom took my brothers and me to the "smelly" market in our small Canadian town, where we strolled among the Eastern European sausage makers, fruit purveyors, and flower ladies. To this day I can't smell hot dogs without picturing that place. These impressions will live vividly in your child's imagination.

- As soon as your boys are old enough, send them to the store for a carton of milk or a dozen eggs. Teach them to check the freshness dates or open the egg carton and look for broken shells.

A Guy-Friendly Pantry

Feeding hungry guys in haste requires a well-stocked cupboard, one full of big flavor items that fill a stomach easily.

A pantry stocked with basics is like your local fast-food restaurant: it's there when you need it, when you can't get to the market and you don't know what to cook. A household kitchen can percolate anytime if some thought has been put into stocking some basic everyday pantry items.

the list

○ **Extra-virgin olive oil:** for value and freshness, buy it in bulk (usually a 3-liter can). Keep a small amount in a cruet or a cleaned bottle, and store the rest in a cool, dark place.

○ **Safflower or other vegetable oil:** safflower is a flavorless, colorless, and healthful oil that tolerates high heat before smoking. Some folks prefer canola, which works well, too.

○ **Vinegars:** red wine, white wine, rice wine, apple cider, and distilled white.

○ **Salt:** coarse kosher salt. Buy a 3-pound box and refill small bowls kept on the countertop and dining table to pinch for easy use.

○ **Black pepper:** buy whole black peppercorns, fill a couple of good grinders, and keep next to the stove and on the dining table.

○ **Red pepper:** dried and crushed red pepper flakes and powdered cayenne pepper.

○ **Herbs and spices:** cinnamon (sticks and ground), nutmeg (whole and ground), cloves (whole and ground), ginger (ground); dried bay leaves, rosemary, thyme, oregano, and paprika.

○ **Canned and dried beans:** black, red, pinto, cannellini, and chickpea. Canned are for quick use, but nothing beats dried beans for value on volume.

○ **Soy sauce:** an average commercial brand or tamari, which has a thicker consistency.

○ **Toasted sesame oil:** once opened, keep refrigerated to prevent a rancid taste.

○ **Tahini sesame paste:** if you plan on making cold sesame noodles, this is a must. Once opened, store the container in the refrigerator.

○ **Fish sauce:** not necessary unless you love Asian food. Several recipes in this book call for it. Look for it in the international section of the grocery store and in Asian food markets.

○ **Worcestershire sauce:** Lea & Perrins is the most widely available brand.

○ **Canned or shelf-stable boxed tomatoes:** whole plum tomatoes. Domestic organic Muir Glen brand consistently has the best tomato flavor. Good-quality imported Italian San Marzano are good (but not always), as are imported Italian tomatoes in a shelf-stable box. Experiment until you find what you like. Taste them before using in a dish. Every recipe can be made from these whether it calls for whole, puréed, or chopped.

○ **Tomato paste:** optional. Buy a tube and keep it refrigerated, which is more economical than a small can since recipes usually require only a couple tablespoons. Many tasty quick dishes can be boosted with this concentrated flavor.

○ **Canned green chilies:** jalapeño or other green chili found in the Mexican section of the grocery store.

○ **Steak sauce:** A1 and/or HP Sauce

- **Dried red chilies:** Mexican ancho, Anaheim red, or New Mexican Hatch, especially if you love to make chili (see page 148).

- **Canned tuna:** white meat packed in water or olive oil (rather than canola oil, if possible). While most people are used to canned tuna, you can get some nice Italian imports in jars.

- **Olives:** basic green and black, preferably bottled for the pantry—but fresh deli varieties will keep for a long time in the fridge.

- **Rice:** basic long-grain such as Carolina. Also, basmati or jasmine for a more fragrant variety if you like cooking Asian dishes. Brown rice is the healthiest but takes longer to cook than white.

- **Pasta:** spaghetti, angel hair (capellini), and macaroni such as penne or rigatoni. Always have two of each, both with the same cooking time, in case you need to cook in volume.

- **Noodles:** long Chinese egg noodles, rice noodles, udon (wheat), and soba (buckwheat).

- **Oats:** best-quality rolled oats, not instant.

- **Raisins:** regular and golden varieties.

- **Nuts and seeds:** walnuts, pecans, sesame seeds, and pine nuts. Once a package has been opened, keep it in the freezer to retain freshness and keep them from becoming rancid, which nuts have a tendency to do.

- **Peanut butter:** natural salted. Store it bottom side up to avoid separation. If used infrequently, keep it refrigerated.

- **Flour:** I prefer unbleached all-purpose flour, but any kind of all-purpose flour will work with the recipes in this book. Store it in the freezer, in an airtight container or resealable plastic bag to avoid a bug infestation.

- **Baking soda and baking powder:** both leaveners for baking; mark the top of the container with the date you opened it, and discard after 6 months. Works best when fresh.

- **Cornstarch:** not mandatory but useful for many things (outside the kitchen, too, such as diaper rash).

- **Sugars:** white, light brown, and confectioners'. If you use sugar often for sweetening tea or coffee, buy organic cane sugar, too.

- **Honey:** an everyday pourable commercial honey. And a minimally processed raw artisanal organic honey loaded with enzymes and other healthful properties. It's worth the expense.

- **Maple syrup:** certified pure real maple syrup.

- **Cocoa:** Dutch-processed unsweetened.

- **Tea:** black and green loose leaves. Also have your favorite commercial tea bags on hand for quick use. Keep a couple of herbal varieties on hand, too, such as mint, chamomile, or rooibos.

- **Coffee:** Dark-roast whole or ground beans from a favorite reputable roaster (such as Illy). And instant espresso for baking.

- **Red and white wine:** anything you'd drink you can cook with.

- **Sparkling water:** keep copious amounts on hand to replace sugary sodas.

- **Mayonnaise:** Hellmann's definitely. Miracle Whip salad dressing if you were raised on it.

- **Ketchup:** Heinz. What else?

- **Mustard:** guys love mustard, so have a few options in the house, such as American neon-yellow, stone-ground, and Dijon.

- **Hot sauce:** Tabasco is the classic.

the measure of the meal: serving sizes

In my house, feeding four big men has meant preparing plenty to eat. But that doesn't translate as just putting a lot on their plates. An overfilled plate can be daunting and off-putting, especially if you're introducing new foods to small kids. Small portions give your guys a manageable meal to consume, and they can always ask for seconds.

HOW TO FEED GUYS

- Always underfill their plates but give more when asked.

- Always figure on more portions than you think. Boys need their fill and are much happier for it. Hungry boys, with not enough food to go around, can be very unpleasant!

- If you cook for a crowd, it's easier to shop for and prepare a few dishes in abundance rather than multiple dishes in smaller quantities.

- Always cook more than you need, so you can keep a steady supply of healthful leftovers in the fridge for later. Leftover dinner for breakfast or lunch is true "fast food" and a much better alternative to the stuff sold at the franchises.

- Don't believe the back of the 16-ounce pasta package that says it makes 8 servings! Cut that estimate at least in half. A pound of pasta feeds no more than four boys.

- The same applies to rice: never make less than 2 cups at a time. Extra rice is a godsend if you're stretching a stew or as a toast alternative at breakfast underneath a fried egg (see page 18)—an easy way to fill hungry morning bellies.

- Increase the volume of all grains, beans, or starches to make meals go further.

Inevitably, with a table full of boys, just when you've fed everyone and tended to the dirty dishes, someone will say he's hungry or another mouth will turn up and ask if there is more food. If you're lucky—and prepared—the answer is yes. And remember, boys will usually eat leftovers before they even have a chance to become leftovers.

MEN LOVE HOT SAUCE

In our totally pepper sauce—obsessed family, the silver platter that sits on our old wooden dining table holds five varieties: Tabasco pepper sauce, Tabasco green pepper sauce, sambal chili paste, sriracha hot chili sauce, and Eve hot pepper sauce—plus, in the kitchen cabinet are Frank's Red Hot Sauce, Jamaican hot pepper sauce, sweet and sour chili sauce, chipotle pepper sauce, papaya pepper sauce, and guayaba pepper sauce.

Hot sauces from all over the world enliven bland foods and enhance already spiced ones. They also satisfy extreme personalities. I like to think the love of hot sauce is synonymous with passion and big, warm characters: you not only taste the heat, you feel it. That sour, spicy balance creates an exciting, dynamic, tangy taste.

Try a couple of dashes ● on a fried egg ● on a golden sautéed pork chop ● over plain rice or chicken ● added to the buttermilk soaking liquid for fried chicken

Manly Jobs
cleaning up

Dishwashing can be a reasonable task or an ongoing nightmare. Teach yourself and your boys and men how to cope with this inevitable burden. If you didn't learn early on to clean up as you go along, please start now. I cannot emphasize this enough: a clean, well-ordered kitchen translates to a tidy, well-ordered mind for cooking.

It's a known, proven, scientifically accurate fact that men simply do not naturally recognize a mess or full garbage even when staring it directly in the face. Set an example. Teach, cajole, and force your boys to clean up after themselves as early and as often as possible. If you don't, they might become that annoying family member, dreaded roommate, or instigator of relationship disaster later. If you've inherited an adult male lacking in cleanup skills, your task is a harder one, but not impossible.

Figure out the best ways to clean and dry the dishes and tidy up the kitchen. Whether you're working in a tiny studio apartment or a big house, ask yourself, "What's the plan?"

Basic cleaning

- Ready the garbage. When it's full (and it always is), someone has to take it out and put in a new garbage bag. As you clean up, debris will need discarding. Set up simple and easily accessible recycling stations: 2 plastic bins: one labeled for paper and one for plastic and glass (these need periodic cleaning, too). Scrape plates before dishwashing.

- Wipe the counter. Keep a clean sponge (and a backup supply), a plastic abrasive scrubber, dish soap, and a couple clean, dry towels at hand.

- Even if you have a dishwasher, fill a bowl or a basin with hot soapy water and put it in the sink. Stick the utensils, dirty side down, in the bowl to soak a little and then wash. It will loosen the dried food for easier cleaning.

- Show your boys how to efficiently load and unload a dishwasher. It doesn't come naturally to them. They think fine crystal glasses are perfectly fine loaded next to a heavy crusted pot, neither of which belongs in a dishwasher. Scrape off food particles and lightly rinse plates then stack side by side, slot after slot in the bottom rack of the dishwasher. Cups and glasses are lined next to each other in the top rack. Don't cram too many utensils into the silverware caddy or the soapy water can't circulate and clean. Start the dishwasher only when it is completely full. Empty the same way you loaded, plates stacked back in the cupboard, glasses, too, and silverware back to their own slots in the silverware drawers. Forks belong with other forks, not with the knives or spoons.

- Boys seem to have a chromosome that enables them to think dry crusted dirty pots and pans will get clean in a dishwasher, even ones that a human being couldn't clean by hand in one try. Really dirty pots and pans must be cleaned by hand. Soak in a little warm, soapy water first. Keep a hard plastic scraping square near the sink to lift the soaked crust off the bottom of the pan, then use the scrubber or sponge, so food bits don't just clump together in the mesh.

> **Boys and men seem to have a chromosome that enables them to think dry crusted dirty pots and pans will get clean in a dishwasher, even ones that a human being couldn't clean by hand in one try.**

Before you start cooking, wash any dirty dishes or you'll dig the hole even deeper. Also, empty the dishwasher or dish drainer in order to make room for the next onslaught. If you were unlucky enough to meet someone else's mess upon entering the kitchen to cook, stay calm. Try to persuade the offender to clean up—or maybe stack the dirty dishes up on his bed, in his sock drawer, or even in his car? If all else fails, quietly and quickly do the dishes yourself, as if practicing a meditation exercise. It never takes as long as you think, and it will save untold mental anguish.

Assign chores to each family member and enforce them. Assign meal cleanup to a different person every night. Or, for each meal, divide the tasks among everyone: table setting, clearing, cleaning, drying, or taking the garbage out. Depending on the age of your kids, tie important privileges to the execution of assigned tasks. Need a ride? Want money? Cell phone? Computer? Not only does spreading the meal chores divide the labor and increase your productivity, it also improves the whole mealtime experience—an essential goal when raising boy eaters and cooks.

Like most kids, I dreaded the whole routine: setting the table, cleaning up after dinner, putting everything away. My mom even made us set the table for breakfast the night before! But my parents never dropped the ball on this uphill battle. So let's not give up on our boys. Clean up as you go along. No exceptions.

Sweeteners

We need to be careful that our palates aren't deadened by the electric sweetness of processed foods. Teach yourself and your menfolk to appreciate natural sweetness. We all love sugar in desserts, but it's hidden in more processed foods than we realize. Sugar is high in calories and devoid of nutrients. Too much sugar contributes to childhood obesity and diabetes. It creates peaks and valleys in their energy level, which creates mood swings, something to teach your guys to avoid. When feeding children, be mindful of how, when, and why you use sugar. Try not to offer sugary snacks to babies and toddlers; they'll find them on their own soon enough. Using sugar and sweets in moderation from a young age is a sound, important practice. Don't deprive yourself or others. But, instead of letting your family have way too much sugar at home, hidden in sodas, cereals, and snacks, you can turn to some pretty amazing substitutes for sweetening.

For baking, of course, its improper balance jeopardizes success. But, for everyday use, consider honey, pure maple syrup, as well as agave, which have organic health benefits. Keep maple syrup and big jars of honey around. Tart citrus such as lemon or grapefruit is delicious with honey. Try different types of honey procured from local markets when traveling. Honey is an essential flavor souvenir of a place. Store a couple of different varieties in your pantry. Its flavor is versatile and always welcome, such as in tea, yogurt, breakfast cereal, snacks, or smoothies.

One of my favorite snacks is plain yogurt mixed with maple syrup, which can be as satisfying as pudding, custard, or ice cream. Many groceries sell large bulk supplies of maple syrup and offer it regularly on sale. A 32-ounce bottle of natural maple syrup can cost as little as twenty dollars. Avoid brands laced with high-fructose corn syrup and other additives.

Keep a large bowl of fresh fruit on the counter in the kitchen, washed and ready to eat. It's likely to be the thing you'll grab on the run. Sure, love your baked dessert or sweet snack, but do so in proportion to the consumption of healthy meals.

Think Aromatic

The challenge of a busy home cook is to maximize flavor with the fewest ingredients. Two of the most important building blocks for the foundation of savory cooking are onions and garlic, though a cook's arsenal of flavor-building blocks depends on the culture or style of the dish being cooked. Shallots, scallions, ginger, tomato paste, anchovies, fresh and dried peppers, spices, and herbs are all excellent ingredients, but mastering and understanding onions and garlic is the starting point for everyday home cooking. Try different varieties of onions; notice the flavor of garlic every time you use it. A mixture that contains onion, garlic, celery, carrot, or other aromatics is called *mirepoix* in French, and *soffritto* in Italian. Cooking with shallots, for example, offers flavor not as sharp as garlic yet with a touch more subtlety than onions. Start to pay attention to these seemingly simple ingredients as you experiment in your cooking. They are the foundations of flavor for soups, sauces, stews, and braises—and also the basis for most of the recipes in this book.

Think for a minute about an onion. It could be yellow, white, or red; pungent and strong or gentle and sweet. Furthermore, each onion on its own has multiple possible flavor stages depending on how it's cooked. Raw, sautéed until translucent, or caramelized are only three of the distinctive taste stages possible from cooking one little onion. Onions eaten raw are best thinly sliced or finely chopped, the powerful flavor experienced in manageable bites. Onions cooked to translucent, for 3 or 4 minutes to soften and mellow as a base for soups or stews, bear little resemblance to caramelized onions achieved by slowly sautéing for 15 to 20 minutes, which produces a rich, caramelized flavor. Purchase onions that are firm to the touch and tightly encased in a dry skin. Choose carefully—a mushy, bruised onion is often sour and bitter.

Stop and think about garlic, too. Its cloves should be firm and plump, snugly encased in their dry papery skin, not shriveled or decayed. Store in a cool, dry place, not in the refrigerator. Raw, sautéed, and roasted garlic each produce completely different outcomes. A peeled and smashed garlic clove can subtly scent a dish before the clove is removed. Or, is the garlic minced raw as a base for salad dressing? Too much can overwhelm with a strong taste. Minced garlic quickly sautéed in heated olive oil results in a mellower version of its terse, raw flavor, but when garlic has been gently browned to light golden, a nuttiness comes out. Wrapped in foil and slow-roasted in the oven, garlic transforms into a delicate sweet savory paste, easily swapped for butter on a piece of bread.

The way you cut garlic and onion makes a difference. If a recipe calls for finely chopped onion, chances are that large pieces, carelessly chopped, won't contribute the right flavor note or look very pleasant. Large chunks of undercooked garlic can be an unwelcome encounter. So can finely minced garlic burned over too high heat.

breakfast

the virtue of a thankless task

All the things they say about breakfast are true. If you eat it, you won't be really starving at noon, and you won't want to eat too much garbage throughout the day. Your metabolism will stay steady, making your performance better and your personality and disposition more agreeable.

make boys eat breakfast

Brainwash them; it works. Tell them they'll be smarter, have fewer zits, anything. Breakfast can be a real problem, especially on school days. Few kids know they're hungry that early in the morning, especially with everyone rushing to get out the door. Frankly, it can be a big drag for the heads of household, who also have to wake everyone up, maybe walk and feed the dog, and ready themselves for work. On top of that, making a breakfast that no one wants and everyone often complains about is truly thankless. But don't expect a boy to make it for himself until you show him how to do it and why it's important.

train him to do it

Aside from teaching guys the importance of eating breakfast by preparing it regularly, train them to help organize it, too. When they begin to fend for themselves, they'll have good habits. Start as soon as possible, asking others in the household to help with the simple tasks of preparing breakfast. Fill the cereal bowls, get out the glasses, napkins, juice, and milk. Put the coffee or tea kettle on. Make it mandatory to eat breakfast before leaving the house, and don't give them money for junk food from elsewhere, which costs more and isn't nutritious. But you have to make breakfast easy to eat, so have the supplies on hand and easily available to prepare.

plan ahead

Don't become a short-order cook—leave that for a restaurant. It's hard enough to pull off one meal a day let alone two or three. So, figure out the night before how to handle the next morning. Take into account how many people are home, whether it's a school morning or a leisurely weekend with guests, and what supplies are in the house. These are all questions better answered in advance instead of facing a group of starving people in the morning with no plan or supplies.

Make only one breakfast. And make enough of it.

- **Cereal:** Select a whole grain. Let your family choose among several healthful varieties and keep them in stock. Put out a couple of choices. Ready the bowls and spoons. Make sure you have milk (make it organic, if possible). Get them to try plain yogurt mixed with honey or maple syrup as a milk alternative. The cereal is mixed with yogurt rather than floated in milk.
- **Portable breakfast:** Spread peanut butter on rice cakes the night before and wrap it. Cut up fruit such as orange or grapefruit wedges and place in a plastic bag. Chill down water. Make sure you have transport supplies: bags, cooler, thermoses, and plastic containers. Don't forget napkins.
- **Pancakes:** Make the batter the night before. Fry all the pancakes at once in the morning; reheat as required by quickly zapping them in the microwave. Get the syrup and butter out. Stack the plates, forks, and napkins the night before. This may seem like overkill, but every detail organized in advance means getting food on the table faster, before you lose the guys to other activities. Unfed, they will return "starving" at the most inopportune time.

What to feed them in the morning

- A bowl of whole-grain cereal with a sliced banana.
- Oatmeal (make it tasty and dress with pure maple syrup).
- A bowl of berries (pick through and discard the mushy ones) and milk.
- Hard-boiled eggs. Cook a half dozen and keep refrigerated. Teach the little kids to crack and peel them. Serve with salt and pepper.
- A fried egg over heated leftover rice. (While the rice heats in the microwave, fry the egg.)
- Scrambled eggs and whole-wheat toast.
- A bowl of their favorite leftover soup or stew from dinner.
- Sliced leftover turkey in pita bread.
- A toasted tortilla with melted cheese.
- Smoothies, smoothies, smoothies.

Water, water everywhere: Make sure there are plenty of healthful liquids available at breakfast, especially water. This is the time to get hydrated for the day. Kids don't yet know this but you do.

- Buy a filtering water pitcher. Keep it full and clean. Train the boys to refill it!
- If you put out juice, make it good juice with no added sugars, artificial colors, or chemicals.
- Squeeze fresh citrus if you can.
- Make a big batch of herbal tea and serve it hot or cold.
- Make smoothies out of frozen fruits and bananas.

For daily breakfast, something decent is better than nothing at all. Eventually your kids will know why it's important because they will feel and see the difference themselves. Just keep harping on it. Eat breakfast yourself—the same one you put out for others. Teach them as boys: eating breakfast daily is much harder for men to pick up themselves later on.

bacon, egg, and cheese sandwich, new york city deli style

makes 1

As most city parents know, at an all-too-early age, your kids rush out in the early morning on their way to school. You beg them to eat breakfast first but instead, if anything, they stop before school at the bagel shop or snack truck for fast food. When I watched our oldest son and his friend spend their entire junior year in high school perfecting a bacon, egg, and cheese breakfast sandwich to rival that of their favorite deli version, a lightbulb went off: replicate the sandwich, wrap it just right in parchment or foil, and hand each boy a portable breakfast as he heads out the door in the morning. As I learned from the boys, the magic combination is two eggs, not scrambled (but yolk broken), with melted cheese on each egg, served on a lightly buttered, griddled (not toasted) "everything" bagel.

1 everything bagel, or bagel of choice

1 tablespoon unsalted butter

2 large eggs

1 thin slice cheese, such as American or cheddar

2 to 3 slices cooked bacon

Hot sauce and/or ketchup, for serving

1 Slice the bagel in half. Butter the halves and toast them in a toaster oven (or use a griddle if you have one). If using a regular pop-up toaster, butter the halves after they're toasted. Meanwhile, heat a cast-iron or nonstick skillet.

2 Add the remaining butter to the skillet. Carefully crack in both eggs. As soon as the whites set up on the bottom, puncture the yolks. Place a slice of cheese on one egg and top with the bacon. Place the other egg, yolk side down, on top of the bacon (like an egg-on-egg sandwich). Lift the whole egg pile onto one toasted bagel half. Top with the other half of the bagel and lightly press together. Serve immediately or wrap halfway in parchment or foil. Douse with hot sauce or dip in ketchup for maximum effect. *

Abbreviated breakfast sandwich If you're in a hurry and your guys are about to run out the door, pile a couple of scrambled eggs on a toasted and buttered roll. Sprinkle on some salt and pepper, wrap in foil or parchment, and tuck a bit of paper towel in one of the outside seams. Put it in their backpacks or hand them off as they go.

Quick bacon When you have some extra time, cook a pound or two of bacon. If you are cooking a lot of bacon, bake it in the oven [see page 45]. If pressed for time and making a smaller amount, use a skillet, but pay close attention since bacon goes from barely cooked to burned very easily.

Drain, cool, and wrap in plastic, three strips per package. Freeze and pull out as needed for a quick breakfast or sandwich. Ten seconds in the microwave or a minute in a preheated pan and the bacon is ready to use.

Bagels Buy fresh bagels in quantity when possible. As soon as you get home, cut each one in half, place the two halves in a sealed bag, and freeze immediately. Optimum freshness will be preserved, and frozen bagel halves can go straight into the toaster—a much better alternative to day-old dry bagels or whole bagels you have to defrost before toasting.

One caution: Beware the poppy seed bagel—it sheds its seeds in the freezer after a boy rips the bag, which one inevitably will do.

the many uses of tortillas

Tortillas, a daily staple of Mexican life, are also a godsend to the rest of us for making healthy fast food. They're among the most versatile, quick snack items you can have in the fridge. They can be rolled around a filling, toasted flat as a platform, cut and fried as a chip, ripped bit by bit to sop up sauce, or layered for a casserole, and they work equally well as a savory or a sweet.

I especially love corn tortillas—so much so that I learned to make my own and did so for many years. For the enthusiastic cook, it's like baking your own bread—a cost-saving and engaging task that produces delicious, economical results. If you have the desire and time to explore, try it. Cookbook author Diana Kennedy gives detailed instructions in *The Art of Mexican Cooking*. Fortunately, for every day, good-quality packaged tortillas are available everywhere.

I've tried many options but the best way to heat **tortillas** is to toast them first, then stack and steam them. Toast one at a time, preferably directly on a gas flame, or in a skillet for about 40 seconds per side, until the edges start to darken. Some will puff up once you turn them over. Even if they toast too firm, stack them on top of each other and wrap the stack in a clean cotton kitchen towel. They will steam gently and become pliable. To keep them fresh for half an hour, wrap the stack tightly in foil and hold in a warm place.

Flour tortillas, which are larger and generally more pliable than corn tortillas, are used in burritos or as a "wrap." They also are good for homemade tortilla chips (as are corn), which are simply tortillas cut in pieces and fried in an inch of hot oil until golden, drained, and sprinkled with salt. (They can also be oven-fried by placing them on a baking sheet brushed with some oil at 450°F for 10 minutes.)

Among the countless instant quick bites you can make with tortillas:
- Toast, slather with butter, and lightly sprinkle with salt.
- Butter, sprinkle with sugar and cinnamon, and toast in a toaster oven.
- Toast, then slather with peanut butter and honey.
- Melt cheese on top of one or between two. Even if only a small heel of dried-out cheese is left in the fridge, grate it on a tortilla, melt, and shake on a few dribbles of hot sauce.
- Layer like lasagna with cheese, shredded chicken, and green sauce (see page 176) and bake in a 375°F oven for 30 minutes.
- Grill with bananas and melted chocolate on top, for dessert.
- Cut in strips, toast, and float on top of chicken soup.
- Serve toasted instead of bread with morning eggs.

breakfast burrito

makes 6 burritos

Hungry boys need to be fed before they become "mad hungry." When the day ahead is an active and long one, it helps to begin with a substantial meal.

This is an easy breakfast to execute if you are heading out for a road trip early in the morning and are determined to avoid feeding the guys overpriced fast food on the road. With a little planning, breakfast burritos and lunch can be prepared and packed up before leaving. Shop a day ahead. Prepare the ingredients and set up the coffeemaker the night before. In the morning you'll need no more than 10 minutes to get this breakfast burrito in the bag.

6 large flour tortillas

2 small smoked chorizo sausages (or linguiça or other cured pork sausages), chopped

10 large eggs, lightly beaten

8 ounces Monterey Jack cheese, grated

⅓ cup prepared salsa (I like Muir Glen black bean and corn salsa)

Hot sauce (optional)

1 Preheat the oven to 300°F. Lay the tortillas on a baking sheet. Place in the oven for 1 minute.

2 Fry the chorizo in a hot pan for 1 minute, then add the eggs and scramble. Meanwhile, sprinkle cheese over each tortilla. Return the tortillas to the oven and allow the cheese to melt, about 1 minute. Remove from the oven.

3 Divide the eggs and sausage evenly among the tortillas, piling the eggs and sausage in the center. Top each one with a tablespoon of salsa and drizzle with hot sauce, if using.

4 One at a time, fold the bottom edge of each tortilla up and over the eggs and sausage, fold in each side edge to form an open pocket, then fold down that edge. If not eating immediately, wrap tightly in foil. ✳

Cured Pork Sausage Chorizo, linguiça, salami, and pepperoni are all smoked or cured spicy pork sausages, Spanish-style chorizo is smoked, but Mexican-style chorizo is made with fresh pork and must be cooked. A little of any of these sausages, minced and added to eggs, beans, soups, and stews, delivers a piquant bottom flavor that is deep and stimulating. Cut and fried, they make a full savory base for simple ingredients like eggs, rice, or pasta, making them taste more complex than they are. Frankly, even hot dogs or bologna could play the same role. They keep in the fridge for a long time and can even be frozen—cut or crumble into serving portions first so you can defrost as needed.

mexican egg scramble

serves 6

For anyone on the go, this is a hearty, portable breakfast—eggs wrapped in tortilla and twisted up in foil on the fly have satisfied my boys for twenty years. At home, just place the pan with the eggs and toasted corn tortillas in the center of the table. Everyone can make their own taco at the table or just use the tortillas as a fork-shovel. Alternatively, salted tortilla chips also make a crunchy contrast to the soft eggs, crumbled over the top. I *love* these eggs very spicy, but the chilies can be adjusted to taste. If you're cooking for one, use two eggs and adjust the other ingredients accordingly.

18 corn tortillas or 1 bag salted tortilla chips

1 tablespoon vegetable oil

5 scallions (both white and green parts), chopped, or ½ cup chopped onion

4 to 6 serrano or jalapeño chilies, minced

1 large or 2 small tomatoes, coarsely chopped

1¼ teaspoons coarse salt

¼ cup chopped fresh cilantro (optional)

1 dozen large eggs

1 If using corn tortillas, toast individually over a gas flame on low or in a pan for about 40 seconds per side. Stack on top of each other and wrap in foil or a clean kitchen towel. This will steam the toasted tortillas for pliability.

2 Heat a 14-inch skillet and then add the oil and swirl it around in the pan. Stir in the scallions and chilies. Add the tomatoes, salt, and cilantro, if using. Stir over high heat for about 2 minutes.

3 Crack the eggs one at a time into the skillet and stir. Cook just until the eggs are set, 1 to 2 minutes. Serve immediately: scoop a portion of eggs onto each plate and offer 3 tortillas each, or crumble tortilla chips over the egg mixture. *

Hot Green Mexican Chilies

● Small jalapeño peppers are available in the produce sections of many supermarkets, and some stores group them together with salsa and guacamole ingredients (cilantro, tomatoes, and avocados). The heat level can vary wildly—some peppers are bred to have no heat at all—so it pays to buy a couple of extra ones and taste before using. The seeds contain most of the heat and can be removed to cool things off.

● On the other hand, the less ubiquitous but more and more available serrano pepper is always hot. I buy a handful for under a dollar, whenever I see good ones. Narrower, smaller, and a lighter green color than jalapeños, serranos are really spicy, and I use them when I want a powerful green chili flavor and heat, even for Asian dishes if neccessary.

● With a small patch of soil, even the most inexperienced of us gardeners can easily grow these chilies with the right light or in a container on a windowsill. If you have an abundance of fresh chilies, seed them, grind them up, wrap in small packages, and freeze. They won't retain their beautiful color, but they will do fine in a cooked dish where their flavor and heat are required.

● Both jalapeños and serranos are available in cans as well, packed in a vinegary *escabeche* liquid. The flavor is more acidic than the fresh, but it will still add the savory heat needed in many dishes. When you see them in the store, buy a few cans for the pantry.

spanish frittata

serves 6 to 8

A Spanish tortilla—*tortilla española,* in Spanish—looks like a large flat omelet. It's absolute perfection in its simplicity and use of minimal ingredients: eggs, potato, salt, onion (some authentic recipes omit the onion), and olive oil—a perfect dish for a big family. In Spain, these tortillas are consumed daily in tapas bars and around the family table as breakfast, lunch, and dinner staples. They're equally delicious served either warm or at room temperature.

My recipe is a hybrid, combining the ingredients of a tortilla with the technique and appearance of a frittata, where the cooking is finished in the oven. We make them in all our cast-iron skillets— 6-, 10-, 12-, and 14-inchers—depending on the size of the group we're feeding. The first one up in the morning prepares the tortilla and leaves it to sit on the stove throughout the day. The boys can grab a wedge on their own time. Sometimes when baked potatoes are on the dinner menu, I'll make extra in anticipation of breakfast the next morning.

For the traditional Spanish tortilla method, use a nonstick skillet. When the eggs are almost set, use a large plate to flip and invert the tortilla onto the plate, then slide it back into the pan to finish cooking.

2 tablespoons extra-virgin olive oil

½ onion, chopped (¾ cup)

1 large potato, peeled, cooked, and cut into ½-inch cubes

1½ teaspoons coarse salt

8 large eggs, beaten

1 Preheat the broiler.

2 Heat a 12-inch cast-iron or nonstick ovenproof skillet over medium heat. Swirl in the olive oil. Add the onion and sauté until translucent, about 3 minutes. Add the potato and ¾ teaspoon of the salt. Continue to cook and occasionally stir until the onion and potato are slightly browned, 5 to 6 more minutes.

3 Add the eggs and the remaining ¾ teaspoon salt. Swirl them around the pan and lower the heat. When the eggs are set on the side but the top is still loose, place the pan under the broiler for 2 minutes. The tortilla will turn slightly golden and puff up before it settles. Cut into wedges to serve. ✳

Leftover Potatoes If baked potatoes are on the menu, cook a few extra to use: ● cubed in a Spanish tortilla ● as filling for an omelet ● grated and fried for hash browns ● mashed and spiced to fill toasted tortillas

eggs poached in tomato sauce

serves 4 to 6

This poached-egg dish makes a great breakfast or brunch, or—as I discovered in a pinch—a quick dinner. One day at work, my boss (Martha Stewart) brought in fresh eggs from her farm. I took a dozen home, thinking I'd use them for breakfast the next morning. When I got home, everyone was starving for dinner, and aside from some basic pantry ingredients and these amazing eggs, there were very few ingredients in the house. After finding some bread in the freezer and spinach in the refrigerator, I served the eggs over toasted bread, with tomato sauce and steamed spinach on the side.

1 28-ounce can whole plum tomatoes or crushed or puréed tomatoes

1 tablespoon olive oil

2 garlic cloves, minced

Pinch of crushed red pepper flakes

Coarse salt and freshly ground black pepper

6 large eggs

6 slices toasted or grilled country bread, for serving

Freshly grated Parmesan cheese, for serving

1 Transfer the tomatoes and their juices to the jar of a blender. Blend until the tomatoes are coarsely chopped.

2 Heat a small skillet over medium-high heat, and then add the olive oil. Quickly add the garlic and red pepper flakes; cook, stirring, until the garlic is lightly golden, about 30 seconds. Add the tomatoes and bring to a boil; season with salt and pepper. Reduce the heat to a simmer and cook for 20 minutes.

3 Gently crack the eggs into the tomato mixture, cover, and let cook for 5 minutes. Remove the skillet from the heat, uncover, and let stand for 2 to 3 minutes. Transfer each egg to a piece of toast. Spoon the sauce over the eggs, garnish with cheese, and season with salt and pepper; serve immediately. ∗

Destined for a lunch box, a sandwich made on frozen bread will defrost by lunchtime and prolong freshness as it stays cold longer.

Freezing Bread

Super-fresh bread, frozen immediately and defrosted later, can be as close to fresh-baked as you can get, and it's much better than day-old bread. This is especially helpful if you live far from a source for good baked bread. Wrapping it well is key: Slice or cube the bread as needed, wrap in plastic wrap, and wrap again in foil. Label with a date. The same is true for packaged sandwich bread: slices pulled from a frozen loaf take only a few seconds to defrost in the microwave or can go straight into the toaster.

omelet for one

makes 1 8-inch omelet

One of the most important things I learned at my first cooking job was how to make an omelet. I was taught to use a well-seasoned pan with a long handle, to cook over the proper heat and to constantly shake the pan, and to whisk the eggs with a fork—just enough to incorporate enough raw egg into the rapidly solidifying cooked egg—without scraping through to the bottom of the pan. To this day, I use my 8-inch classic French Bon Chef heavy aluminum omelet pan, which I purchased in 1976.

If you're a novice at omelets, you might prefer an 8-inch pan made of stainless steel with a nonstick finish, sloping sides, a flat bottom, and a long handle. Once you get the method down, the whole process from whisking the eggs to folding the omelet onto the plate shouldn't take more than 5 minutes.

3 large eggs

2 teaspoons water

Large pinch of coarse salt

1½ teaspoons unsalted butter

Filling of choice, such as grated or shredded cheese, herbs, chopped vegetables, sliced cooked bacon, or diced ham

1 Whisk together the eggs, water, and salt. Heat a well-seasoned (or nonstick) 8-inch skillet over high heat, about 30 seconds.

2 Add the butter. It should bubble but not smoke and burn. (If it does burn, wipe out the butter and start over.) Swirl the butter around the pan and immediately pour in the eggs. When the eggs begin to turn opaque around the edges, use a heat-proof plastic spatula to pull the cooked eggs away from the sides of the pan. Swirl the pan to fill in the opening with the uncooked eggs. Reduce the heat to medium low. Repeat swirling until the omelet's underside is set all around and the top is still slightly undercooked. Starting from the middle, place any filling in the omelet.

3 Ready a plate, warmed in a low oven or under hot water. Fold one third of the omelet over the filling, away from the handle side of the pan. Using a spatula, loosen the bottom of the omelet. Holding the pan with your palm under the handle, slide the unfolded edge onto the plate. As it slides off the edge of the pan, use the edge of the pan to help flip the ⅔ folded portion over the unfolded ⅓ portion on the plate. You'll form a roll with the seam on the bottom. Serve immediately. ⋆

perfect fried egg every time
makes 1 egg

How many times have you had a fried egg with a tough, chewy white? Or, conversely, my least favorite version, a white that is overcooked on the bottom and gooey on top? This technique, which steams the top of the egg while cooking it from the bottom, works best. For several eggs, use a larger skillet.

½ teaspoon unsalted butter

1 large egg

1 teaspoon water

Salt and freshly ground black pepper

Heat a small cast-iron or nonstick skillet over medium-high heat. Add the butter and swirl it to coat the skillet. Immediately crack the egg into the skillet. Add the water to the pan, reduce the heat to medium low, cover, and cook for 1 minute. Remove the egg from the pan immediately. Season to taste with salt and pepper and serve. *

Buying and Using Eggs Eggs are a high-protein, versatile ingredient for any meal. They are one of the few ingredients (chicken and milk are two others) that I always buy organic. Reducing the consumption of hormones by boys seems right; they already have enough! If price is a consideration, I think you should scrimp elsewhere. Try to purchase eggs from a farmers' market whenever you can. In the supermarket, I prefer cage-free eggs from naturally raised chickens; devoid of antibiotics and hormones, these eggs are tastier and more healthful. Brown, beige, white, or blue—all eggs have the same flavor. Flavor and texture are determined by freshness rather than by color of shell or type of chicken. The white of a fresh egg holds together when cooked instead of being watery and loose. A fresh yolk will be a deep yellow to almost orange, preferable to a pale yellow one. Still, any supermarket egg eaten within the sell-by date is a good food source for a busy home cook.

Most recipes assume the use of large eggs. Extra-large eggs can be substituted unless you are baking or making pastry, in which case the added volume will change the outcome. If you keep eggs in the fridge, the potential quick-meal options are endless: omelet; Spanish tortilla; frittata; taco; egg sandwich; scrambled, fried, soft-boiled, and hard-boiled egg; and poached egg on toast, to name a few.

golden granola

makes 2 quarts

So many commercially made granolas are laced with sweetener and unwanted trans-fatty acids. They are just plain yucky and easily go rancid by the time you buy them off the shelf. A homemade version is very simple to make and worth the effort. Not only don't men and boys believe in eating breakfast, but they need to be convinced about the value of nutrients such as fiber, protein, and good carbs found in grains, nuts, and fruits. They will like homemade granola with its satisfying crunchy texture and sweet and savory flavors, as long as there aren't too many weird ingredients.

1 pound rolled oats

1 cup shredded, unsweetened coconut (or sweetened, if you prefer)

½ cup slivered almonds

¼ cup sesame seeds

½ cup wheat germ

½ teaspoon coarse salt

½ cup safflower oil

½ cup honey

⅓ cup water

1½ teaspoons pure vanilla extract

½ cup golden raisins

½ cup dried cranberries, blueberries, or other dried chopped fruit

1 Preheat the oven to 250°F.

2 In a large bowl, toss together the oats, coconut, almonds, sesame seeds, wheat germ, and salt. Separately whisk together the oil, honey, water, and vanilla; stir it into the oat mixture.

3 Spread the granola on 2 rimmed baking sheets. Bake for 1 to 1½ hours, or until golden brown. Stir after 10 minutes and again after 30 more minutes. Remove from the oven and toss with the raisins and cranberries. Cool completely and store in an airtight container. Serve with sliced bananas or berries and milk or plain yogurt. *

Keeping Cereal Fresh Guys will rip open the bags within the cereal box and neglect to roll them shut. Usually the box tab is also ripped off. Here are a few tips. ● Transfer the contents to a resealable bag and return to the cereal box. ● Store the cereal in an airtight plastic or metal container. Try a recycled takeout container. ● To recrisp softened granola, spread on a baking sheet, oven-bake for 10 minutes at 350°F, and cool.

Shredded coconut ● Dry, unsweetened is available in most health food stores. ● Homemade: Crack open a dry, brown coconut. Drain. Pry the flesh from the shell with a dull knife (brown skin OK to leave on) and shave into pieces with a potato peeler. ● Packaged shredded and naturally sweetened coconut is acceptable, too.

creamy spiced oatmeal

serves 4

My experience feeding boys has taught me that oatmeal is the most efficient breakfast for long-term morning energy. After all these years, I've convinced the boys, too, one of whom started asking for it when any sort of school test loomed. But oatmeal can be boring and tasteless if not prepared properly. Try using milk, steeped with spices, and the best-quality oats. Vary the "sweet spices"— such as cinnamon, cloves, nutmeg, ginger, allspice, coriander, and star anise—to taste or according to what's in your cupboard. Top with maple syrup or honey, sliced bananas, and maybe some chopped toasted almonds. Save time on busy weekday mornings by making a large pot of oatmeal on Sunday night, then cooling and storing it in the refrigerator in a large covered container. Reheat the needed quantity in a saucepan or microwavable bowl, stirring in a little water or milk to loosen up the cereal.

1 cup milk (soy, almond, or rice milk can be substituted)

½ cup water

1 whole cinnamon stick

3 whole cloves

4 allspice berries (optional)

1 bay leaf

1 cup rolled oats, preferably organic

½ cup pure maple syrup or honey

2 ripe bananas (optional)

½ cup toasted almonds (optional)

1 In a medium saucepan, heat the milk and water with the spices and bay leaf over medium heat. Reduce the heat to low and steep for 2 minutes. Add the oats and cook, stirring occasionally, until the oats are tender, between 5 and 15 minutes.

2 Remove from the heat and cover for a minute. Discard the bay leaf and whole spices. Portion into bowls and drizzle with maple syrup, then top with the bananas and almonds, if desired. Serve immediately. ∗

Oats A half-cup serving of heart-healthy, whole-grain oats contains seven B vitamins; many minerals, including iron and calcium; cholesterol-lowering water-soluble fiber; and 6 grams of protein. Many types of oats are available. Look for oats with texture and body. ● Steel-cut oats are oat groats cut into two or three pieces but not rolled before drying, requiring a long cook time to become tender. ● Thick, old-fashioned rolled oats, which will cook a little more quickly than steel-cut, are oat groats steamed and flattened with huge rollers, then dried. ● Don't buy the mushy instant variety consisting of cut oat groats, precooked and dried before rolling, which contain the least nutrition of the three types and are often sold presweetened and artificially flavored. ● Regardless of the package instructions, ask yourself if you like your oatmeal thick or thin, chewy or soft, sweet or savory, then experiment with the liquid to grain ratio, cooking time, and flavoring until you have your favorite consistency. This recipe results in a thick and creamy dish.

old-fashioned pancakes

makes 2 cups batter; 16 4-inch pancakes

This is the most basic recipe for a slightly thick pancake. It's just as easy to make a quick homemade batter as it is to open a box mix, which needs ingredients added to it anyway. And using organic ingredients seems to give the pancakes a cleaner and truer flavor. Get the kids involved in the preparation when they're young. It may turn out to be their only cooking skill, but it's one worth having. Also known as hotcakes, griddle cakes, and flapjacks, pancakes are a very economical way to feed an army of ravenous boys. A couple of strips of bacon, a few sausage links, and a fried egg on top is the best home-style rendition of the classic diner offering. Cook up the whole recipe of batter, even if not all the pancakes are needed for breakfast. Serve the leftovers for snacks or dinner, with peanut butter, honey, or jam spread on top. Or, cook a lumberjack special for dinner!

I always use unbleached all-purpose flour; it's available in most grocery stores and markets.

1½ cups all-purpose flour

1 tablespoon sugar

1 teaspoon coarse salt

2¾ teaspoons baking powder

1 large egg, lightly beaten

1¼ cups milk

3 tablespoons unsalted butter, melted, plus more for serving

Vegetable oil, for the griddle

Pure maple syrup, warmed, for serving

1 Place a heat-proof platter into a warm oven (at 200°F).

2 In a large bowl, whisk together the flour, sugar, salt, and baking powder. Make a well in the center of the flour mixture. Add in the egg, milk, and 2 tablespoons of the butter. Whisk from the center, slowly incorporating the flour. Rest the batter for 10 minutes.

3 Heat a large well-seasoned cast-iron skillet or favorite griddle over medium-high heat. Swirl the remaining tablespoon of butter in the skillet (or use oil to coat the griddle) and immediately pour in ¼ cup of batter for each pancake. When bubbles rise to the surface, flip the pancakes, slightly reduce the heat, and cook until the bottoms are golden and the centers are cooked, about 1 minute. (Rarely does the first pancake work because it takes a bit of time to get in the groove with the heat, fat, and batter.)

4 As the pancakes come out of the skillet, place them on the warm platter in the oven until ready to serve. Serve a stack of 3 pancakes, topped with more butter and the maple syrup. *

Pancakes Add-ins

● Mash a ripe banana and mix it into the batter. ● Fold in ¾ cup of berries. Blueberries are especially good with banana batter. ● Sauté thinly peeled, cored, and sliced apples in a little butter with a dash of cinnamon. Spoon onto the uncooked side of the pancakes before flipping. ● Replace half of the all-purpose flour with whole-wheat, buckwheat, or rye flour. ● Toast pecans or walnuts, chop, and fold them into the batter. Slice fruit on top of the pancake before flipping.

man crepes

makes 12 crepes

Our city boys grew up eating crepes from curbside vendors at local street fairs. They still love those fat crepes with their cloyingly sweet filling. At home you can do a lot better by making them a little thinner, served with just a sprinkling of sugar and a squeeze of lemon or orange juice, for breakfast, lunch, a snack, or dessert.

Back in my catering days, we made hundreds and served them in place of the noodle for baked cannelloni, filled with cheese and topped with tomato sauce (page 179). Crepe batter will keep well in the fridge overnight should you wish to prepare it in advance or have any left over. Or, cook all the batter, stack the crepes, and wrap them in plastic wrap. The crepes will hold in the refrigerator for 2 or 3 days. You can stuff, roll, and bake them with sauce or cheese for another preparation. The varieties of fillings are endless, from fruit to cheese and meat.

¾ cup all-purpose flour

½ teaspoon coarse salt

1 teaspoon baking powder

3 large eggs

⅔ cup milk

⅓ cup water

½ teaspoon pure vanilla extract

Unsalted butter, for frying and spreading

Sugar, for sprinkling

Wedges of oranges or lemons, for squeezing

1 Heat an ovenproof platter in a warm (200° F) oven.

2 Place the flour, salt, baking powder, eggs, milk, water, and vanilla in a blender and blend until completely combined and the consistency of heavy cream. The batter can be refrigerated up to 1 day in advance.

3 Heat a well-seasoned 6-inch skillet or crepe pan until very hot to the touch but not smoking. Swirl around enough butter to coat the pan. Gently and slowly pour a 3- or 4-tablespoon portion of batter, immediately swirling to cover the entire bottom of the pan in as thin a layer as possible. When the edges begin to turn golden and pull away from the pan, use a spatula to lift and flip the crepe. Cook until it is just set, about 30 seconds. Repeat until the batter is finished, stacking the crepes on the platter in the oven as you go. Serve immediately with some butter, sugar, and a squeeze of citrus. *

sour cream waffles

makes 3 or 4 large (7 x 7-inch) waffles; serves 4 to 6

Waffles are always a winner and the only complaint you'll hear is that you're not making them fast enough for the pack of hungry boys. So fire up the waffle iron and prepare for the clamor. Prepare your toppings first so you can keep the waffles rolling without pause. This recipe makes an eggy waffle—in a Scandinavian style. My middle son likes to make his own topping: 1 part honey to 3 parts maple syrup, whisked together with 3 tablespoons melted butter. A combination of melted chocolate, whipped cream, and berries turns the waffle into another beloved and impressive treat.

5 large eggs

½ cup sugar

1 cup all-purpose flour

1 teaspoon coarse salt

½ teaspoon ground ginger, cinnamon, or cardamom

1 cup sour cream

4 tablespoons (½ stick) unsalted butter, melted and cooled

Vegetable oil or extra melted butter, for the waffle iron

1 cup berries, fresh or frozen and heated before serving

1 Beat the eggs and sugar together for 5 to 8 minutes. When the beater is lifted, it should trail a ribbon of batter.

2 Whisk together the flour, salt, and spice. With a spoon, alternately fold into the batter half of the flour mixture, the sour cream, and finally the remaining flour mixture. Lightly stir in the melted butter. Let the batter sit for 10 minutes.

3 Heat a nonstick or well-seasoned waffle iron to medium high. Brush lightly with oil or melted butter. Pour in 1¼ cups batter and cook until golden, 2½ to 3 minutes per side for a stovetop waffle iron. An electric waffle iron will beep when ready. Serve with fresh berries or berry sauce on top. *

Waffle Irons

Stovetop or electric? For many years I was happy with my old-fashioned, well-seasoned stovetop waffle iron, which is cast iron and must be carefully cleaned (wiped down with warm water—never soap—and then dried) and also must be turned to properly cook both sides of the waffle. This maneuver can be tricky until you get the hang of it. An electric version has a light to tell you when it is preheated; it beeps when the waffle is cooked, and it has a heating element on both sides, so it doesn't require flipping. This is clearly a much easier appliance to use. Yet, no matter whether your waffle iron is nonstick or not, always spray or wipe on cooking oil or melted butter before pouring batter onto the hot surface.

pear-stuffed french toast

serves 6 to 8

Combining some minced fruit with butter and stuffing it in the center of each piece of French toast transforms this dish into something special to make on a weekend or holiday. Guys love any sweet, battery, eggy bread dish like this even better if partnered with a salty, pork-based breakfast meat of any type. Here, in one bite, you get sweet syrup flowing onto savory meat, joined with the crispy yet creamy French toast.

Use cream, half-and-half, or milk for this recipe. Higher fat content translates into better flavor.

7 tablespoons unsalted butter, softened, plus more for serving

2 pears, peeled, cored, and finely chopped

1 dozen large eggs

2 cups heavy cream, half-and-half, or milk

2 teaspoons pure vanilla extract

1 loaf challah or other soft, thick bread, cut into 1-inch slices

Pure maple syrup, warmed, for serving

1 Mash together 5 tablespoons of the butter with the chopped pears and chill.

2 In a large flat dish, whisk together the eggs, cream, and vanilla.

3 In the side of each bread slice, make a deep slice into the center to form a pocket. Stuff a spoonful of pear butter into each piece. Place the stuffed bread into the egg mixture and let soak for a few minutes. Turn each piece and continue soaking until the bread has absorbed enough of the egg mixture to be completely moistened but not falling apart.

4 Heat a large skillet and swirl in 1 tablespoon of the butter. Working in batches, cook the soaked bread until golden brown and cooked through, 2 to 3 minutes per side. Add the remaining tablespoon of butter to the skillet as needed. Serve warm with more butter and the maple syrup. *

Regular French Toast

Any bread will work for French toast, especially if it's stale—the dryness of stale bread makes it more porous so it readily absorbs the egg mixture. Slightly soften the bread in a microwave, uncovered, for 1 minute, then slice. The French name for this dish is *pain perdu,* literally "lost bread." The original freshness is lost, making it perfect for soaking in egg and frying in butter! You can use old dinner rolls (slice horizontally before soaking) or English muffins. I've used hot dog and hamburger buns in a pinch—even Italian panettone bread from the Christmas holidays.

simple homemade sausage patties

makes 8 small patties

Our family manifesto: Breakfast meat is a must for a weekend or special-occasion breakfast. One weekend morning, I was without sausages or bacon but I did have ground pork for meat loaf in the fridge. Assembling pork sausages is a snap and, as always, if you use best-quality ingredients, it's hard to beat homemade. It's important to be flexible in the kitchen, switching gears on a dime as each meal presents itself.

1 pound ground pork

1 garlic clove, minced

1 tablespoon dried sage, crumbled

¾ teaspoon dried thyme

½ teaspoon dried fennel, crushed

Pinch of ground nutmeg

1½ teaspoons coarse salt

½ teaspoon freshly ground black pepper

1 large egg white

2 teaspoons vegetable oil

1 Mix together the pork, garlic, sage, thyme, fennel, nutmeg, salt, and pepper in a medium bowl. Add the egg white and combine thoroughly. Cover and chill for at least 15 minutes.

2 To easily form the sausage patties, rinse your hands in cold water. Divide the mixture into eighths and shape each portion into a 2½-inch disk. Patties can be made to this point and refrigerated or frozen until ready to use.

3 Heat a skillet over high heat, and then swirl in the oil. Fry the sausages on both sides until completely cooked through and golden brown, about 4 minutes per side. Drain and serve immediately with pancakes, waffles, or eggs. Sausage patties can be fully cooled, wrapped, and frozen for microwave reheating. ✳

Sometimes a home cook's challenge isn't just to make homemade food but also to make do with what you have on hand.

oven-fried bacon

serves 4 to 6

There's no better way to cook a lot of bacon than baking, for both efficiency and cleanup. The bacon doesn't need constant attention in the oven as it does frying on the stove top, leaving you to cook the eggs, pancakes, or French toast at the same time. A rimmed baking sheet, lined with foil, creates a hassle-free aftermath. Drain the grease into a recycled metal tin (an empty coffee can works well) and store covered in the freezer for future use or until it is completely filled and ready for the garbage. Discard the foil and voilà—all that remains is a clean, or easy to wash, baking sheet. A large paper grocery bag also makes an excellent absorbent surface for draining the grease from the cooked bacon.

1 Preheat the oven to 400°F.

2 Lay the bacon strips (one 12-ounce package best quality thick cut) side by side but not overlapping across a rimmed baking sheet. Lay any extra strips perpendicular along the sides. Bake for 15 to 18 minutes, checking periodically to assure even baking. (Thin-cut bacon cooks in 12 to 15 minutes.)

3 Drain the bacon on paper towels or a brown paper bag. Serve immediately or cool and wrap in plastic wrap in individual portions and freeze for future use. ⋆

Never Be Caught Without Bacon

Many guys without dietary or religious restraints (and even some with) regard bacon as their favorite food group. Unless you're a fanatic, in which case you should join the bacon-of-the-month club and taste America's finest artisanal bacons, you're probably buying everyman bacon in the supermarket, which can be tricky with all the choices available these days. A few tips: ● Turn the package over and look through the plastic window to assure proper meat to fat ratio (i.e., not all fat). Check the sell-by date. If you will not be cooking the whole package at one time, store the remainder in the refrigerator for a week or in the freezer for a couple months. Keep a whole unopened pack in the freezer so you're never caught without! ● Thick-cut bacon is meatier but harder to crisp up and requires a longer cooking time. ● Beware of brands that are too salty or loaded with unnecessary extra chemicals. Experiment with a few brands until you find your favorite. I like Oscar Mayer Thick Cut (yes, it has nitrates, but it is inexpensive and tastes good), and Niman Ranch, Nodine's, or D'Artagnan are my choices here for premium commercial varieties.

aunt patty's coffee cake

makes 1 Bundt cake

My godmother's coffee cake would arrive at our house by mail wrapped in foil, almost wet and gooey on the outside and still moist, with the most amazing texture inside. Her trick was wrapping it in foil while it was still hot from the oven, and then freezing it. She put the frozen cake in the mail, and its super-moist texture developed during the trip defrosting. There is something about the coffee and cocoa filling that makes it impossible to stop eating. Serve with coffee or hot chocolate, for breakfast or as a part of a brunch meal. Add a scoop of ice cream and chocolate sauce, and you have dessert.

FILLING

2 tablespoons sugar

1 tablespoon instant coffee

1 tablespoon unsweetened cocoa powder

CAKE

2 cups all-purpose flour

1 teaspoon baking soda

1 teaspoon baking powder

1½ teaspoons coarse salt

8 tablespoons (1 stick) unsalted butter, softened

1 cup sugar

2 large eggs, at room temperature

1 cup sour cream, at room temperature

1 teaspoon pure vanilla extract

Salted versus unsalted butter

I prefer to always use unsalted butter. The sweet cream flavor is subtle and delicious. For buttered toast, you can sprinkle on a little salt—but, in cooking and baking, you can more easily control a dish's overall saltiness by keeping the butter and salt separate. Often salt masks old butter's lack of freshness.

1 Preheat the oven to 350°F. Butter and flour a 12-cup Bundt pan.

2 In a small bowl, mix together the sugar, instant coffee, and cocoa.

3 Separately whisk together the flour, baking soda, baking powder, and salt. Using an electric mixer, cream together the butter and sugar. Add one egg at a time, beating until just combined. Beat in one third of the flour mixture, then half of the sour cream, then another third of the flour mixture. Beat in the remainder of the sour cream and the last third of the flour mixture. (Always start with flour and end with flour.) Add the vanilla and mix for another minute or two, scraping the sides of the bowl well with a spatula.

4 Pour one third of the batter into the prepared pan and sprinkle half of the filling on top. Pour in another third of the batter and sprinkle the remainder of the filling on top of that. End with the last third of the batter. Run a dinner knife down through the batter and swirl the knife gently to marble the batter in about six places.

5 Bake for 50 minutes, or until a cake tester inserted in the middle of the cake comes out clean. Cool on a rack for 30 minutes, then turn out onto a plate or onto foil. The cake can be frozen while still warm. ✳

blueberry bran muffins

makes 12 muffins

A handwritten note on this recipe from 1978 says "best blueberry muffins." I made them dozens and dozens of times at Bims gourmet shop where I worked during that summer. All these years later, I still love this moist muffin, which is healthful as well as enriched with bran and not too sweet. It makes for a quick breakfast and snack or is a great addition to a larger meal. Spread with apricot or peach jam? Delicious.

2 cups all-purpose flour

1 tablespoon baking soda

½ teaspoon coarse salt

2 large eggs

4 tablespoons pure maple syrup

½ cup sugar

½ cup safflower (or other vegetable oil)

1½ cups milk

1 cup fresh or frozen blueberries

½ cup wheat bran or wheat germ

1 Preheat the oven to 400°F. Grease a standard 12-cup muffin tin or line with paper liners.

2 In a large bowl, whisk together the flour, baking soda, and salt. Separately beat together the eggs, maple syrup, sugar, oil, and milk. Stir the egg mixture into the flour mixture. Stir in the berries and bran. Fill the muffin cups three-quarters full.

3 Bake for 25 minutes, or until golden brown. Cool for 5 minutes in the pan before removing. *

Blueberries You can toss the blueberries in flour before adding to the batter, and they will suspend more evenly throughout the muffin instead of sinking to the bottom. If fresh blueberries are unavailable, use frozen instead. Just be sure to fold them in quickly and gently to avoid coloring all the batter blue.

not-your-coffee-shop scones

makes 12 scones

As folks who may have traveled and hitchhiked around the United Kingdom on a skimpy budget know, high tea is a filling and affordable meal, and one that includes scones. The last time I baked scones, my middle son returned home in the morning after sleeping over at a friend's house. The first thing out of his mouth was, "Do you know how amazing it is to come home and smell fresh baking?" I did then. Teatime scones are also a quick baked good to whip up for breakfast. This recipe is very basic and traditional. Serve with butter, Devonshire cream, and jam.

3½ cups all-purpose flour, plus more if needed

2 teaspoons baking powder

1 teaspoon baking soda

1 teaspoon coarse salt

1 cup buttermilk

1 large egg

2 tablespoons sugar, plus more for sprinkling

8 tablespoons (1 stick) unsalted butter, melted, plus more for glazing

⅓ cup currants or other dried fruit, cut into pieces

1 Preheat the oven to 400°F. Butter or line 2 rimmed baking sheets.

2 In a large bowl, whisk together the flour, baking powder, baking soda, and salt. In another large bowl, beat together the buttermilk, egg, and sugar.

3 Stir two thirds of the flour mixture into the buttermilk mixture. Gradually add the melted butter, incorporating it thoroughly into the mixture. Stir in the remaining flour mixture and the currants. The dough should be slightly stiff. Add a little more flour if needed.

4 Turn the dough out onto a clean, well-floured surface and gently knead for under a minute. (Overkneading the dough will make it tough.) Separate the dough into 3 equal parts. Shape each part into a thick 5-inch circle. With a sharp knife, cut the circles into quarters. Arrange the wedges on the prepared baking sheets, spacing them about an inch apart. Brush with some melted butter and generously sprinkle with sugar. Bake for 20 to 25 minutes, until lightly browned on top. Serve warm or at room temperature. ∗

flaky buttery biscuits

makes 12 small biscuits

Fresh hot biscuits slathered with butter, topped with a spoonful of luscious jam, and served alongside fluffy scrambled eggs and a salty pork product are the epitome of a cozy breakfast that will draw any male to your table. They're so versatile because they're equally welcome at breakfast or dinner (think fried chicken), or as the basis for a shortcake dessert (see page 239). They're simple to master, and your family will love you for them. For softer, cakier biscuits, add more milk and spoon the mixture onto the baking sheet. Firmer biscuits require less milk and should be rolled out and cut with a biscuit cutter or the rim of a glass.

1¾ cups all-purpose flour

2½ teaspoons baking powder

1 teaspoon coarse salt

6 tablespoons (¾ stick) chilled unsalted butter, cut into small pieces

¾ cup milk (see headnote)

1 Preheat the oven to 450°F. Butter or line a baking sheet.

2 In a medium bowl, whisk together the flour, baking powder, and salt. Using a fork or 2 table knives, combine the butter and flour mixture until they resemble a coarse meal. Slowly add the milk, stirring with a fork, to the desired consistency.

3 For softer biscuits, drop 2 tablespoons of the dough onto the lined baking sheet. For firmer biscuits, turn the dough out onto a clean, lightly floured surface and gently knead just to bring the dough together. Carefully roll out the dough about ¾ inch thick. Using a biscuit cutter or a sturdy glass, cut about 12 biscuits, rerolling any scraps. Place on the lined baking sheet. (The biscuits can be frozen at this point. Freeze on the baking sheet, then remove to a resealable container or plastic bag for easier storage.) Bake the biscuits for 13 to 15 minutes (add 3 to 4 additional minutes for frozen ones), until golden brown. Cool slightly and serve warm. ∗

frosty banana berry smoothie

makes 2 10-ounce servings

Smoothies make a quick and easy breakfast and they're also a snack that any boy would welcome after school or sports. Bananas, a staple in our fruit bowl, and plain yogurt, always in the refrigerator, form the basis, but the liquid can be varied, its sweetness tweaked, and the berries alternated with raspberry, strawberry, or blackberry. Getting the proportion right—a balance of frozen, creamy, and sweet—is the challenge.

6 ounces plain yogurt

¾ cup fresh or frozen berries
(if using frozen berries, decrease the ice)

1 banana, peeled

½ cup orange juice, preferably fresh squeezed

1 tablespoon pure maple syrup
(or honey, if desired)

1 cup ice cubes

Place all ingredients in a blender jar and blend until smooth. Serve immediately. ∗

Berries Berries frozen at the peak of their ripeness are much tastier than fresh unripe or out-of-season berries, so always have a supply in the freezer. Buy best-quality berries from the grocer's freezer or fresh ones from a farmers' market, or pick your own bumper crop (organic is preferable), then wash and dry the berries and spread them on a rimmed baking sheet. Freeze until each berry is frozen, and gather them together in a resealable plastic bag or container for frozen storage.

Hungry-Boy Snacks One day, after an afternoon soccer game between a sandwich and dinner, my youngest son consumed for a snack, in rapid succession: a full recipe of Cheesy Corn Snack (page 110), a half quantity of Spiced Sweet Potato Wedges (page 198), and a 10-ounce smoothie. It seems like a lot to snack on, but each item was tasty, fresh, and healthful. For a six-foot-tall growing boy, it's a much better alternative than anything artificially processed.

frothy citrus drink

makes 2 8-ounce servings

If you have a little extra time or an abundance of fresh citrus, offer the boys this drink. It's slightly frothy, with a perfect balance of sweet and sour—and of course it's packed with vitamin C. Add a touch of seltzer for a little sparkle.

2 grapefruits

2 oranges

1 lime

3 tablespoons honey

1 Cut the grapefruits, oranges, and lime in half. Juice them with an electric juicer or by hand. Pour the juice into a blender jar. Add the honey and blend on high speed for 30 seconds.

2 Pour into a pitcher and chill before serving. *

SODA OR JUICE ALTERNATIVE

sweet rooibos tea

makes 4 cups

Rooibos tea leaves come from the rooibos ("red bush") plant, which is native to South Africa and known as "bush tea." Widely used in England, the tea is a super-antioxidant herb that has a similar earthy flavor as tea without the caffeine. Prepare a large batch and leave it chilled in the refrigerator as an alternative to soda or juice. It always seems to elevate the spirits.

¼ cup loose rooibos tea

5 cups boiling water

2 tablespoons honey

Pour the boiling water over the dried herbs. Steep for 4 minutes and strain, discarding the leaves. Stir in the honey. Serve hot or chill and serve over ice. *

Soda? Don't Obviously, if you never keep soda at home, your kids won't drink it all the time because it won't be there. Instead, teach them to drink plain and sparkling water and other fresh and delicious beverages, such as fresh, natural juice, cold sweetened herbal infusions, and various milks and nectars. As long as something good is there to quench their thirst, they'll avoid loading their bodies with too much sugar and empty calories. Most sodas are sweetened with high-fructose corn syrup extracted from nutritionless genetically modified corn, which food activist Michael Pollan calls "corncob in a cup." You can't control what's drunk outside of your home. You can help form good habits at home.

Comfort Beverages When someone can't sleep, has a tummy ache, is feeling down, or just needs some attention and you're not sure what else to do, serve a cup of tea. In households where the drinking of fresh-brewed coffee is the morning ritual, offer alternatives such as tea, herbal infusions, or hot chocolate. It's a quiet and soothing way for the gang to start the day.

Herbal Infusions Lots of natural herbs, plants, and fruits—both dried and fresh (and safe and healthy for everyday consumption)—can be steeped in boiled water for a short while (from 5 minutes to an hour), drained, sweetened with honey or maple syrup, and chilled. Store the infusion in a pitcher—something tall, narrow, and colorful that screams "thirst-quenching." Peering into the fridge for a cold drink, the boys in the house will reach for this first.

fresh ginger tea (tisane)

makes 4 cups

Use this to soothe anyone suffering from flu or a cold or upset stomach. It's also delicious with an Asian meal, hot or poured over ice.

¼ cup grated fresh ginger

4 cups boiling water

4 teaspoons honey

Put the grated ginger into a teapot and pour in the boiling water. Allow the mixture to steep for 4 minutes. Strain and serve the tea with a teaspoon of honey in each cup. Stir and serve. *

fresh mint tea

makes 4 cups

When mint is growing wild in your garden, or is available at the green market or produce section, make this herbal brew. It's a comforting way to start the day or end a meal. It's also a wonderful complement to most desserts as well as a settler of queasy stomachs.

12 large sprigs of fresh mint

4 cups boiling water

4 teaspoons honey

Wash the mint and place it in a large heat-proof pitcher. Pour the boiling water over the mint and allow it to steep for 4 minutes. Strain and serve with a teaspoon of honey in each cup. Or, return the strained tea to the pitcher. Stir in the honey and chill. *

CLOCKWISE FROM TOP: Sweet Rooibos Tea (page 54), Fresh Ginger Tea (this page), Fresh Mint Tea (this page)

spiced chai latte

makes 4 cups

Spiced chai latte is a hybrid name, popularized in our fancy coffee-shop culture. *Chai,* an East Indian word for tea, and *latte,* Italian for milk, blend together with aromatic spices for a flavorful, exotic beverage that tastes of spice cake. Boys and men appreciate this satisfying pick-me-up both morning and afternoon.

2 tablespoons black tea

3 whole cloves

1 star anise (or other aromatic spice)

1 whole cinnamon stick

4 cups boiling water

½ teaspoon pure vanilla extract, or ½-inch piece of vanilla bean

1 tablespoon natural sugar or honey

¼ cup hot milk

Put the tea, cloves, star anise, and cinnamon stick in a teapot or heat-proof pitcher. Add the boiling water and let steep for 3 to 4 minutes. Strain the tea into 4 cups. Stir in the sweetener and hot milk and serve. *

hot chocolate

makes 6 cups

You can buy any number of mixes for hot chocolate, but even something this simple is so much tastier and also better for you if made from scratch using the best ingredients on hand. Serve for breakfast in the morning or for a delicious treat any time, with miniature marshmallows floating on top.

6 tablespoons best-quality Dutch-processed cocoa powder (or whatever unsweetened cocoa you have on hand)

6 tablespoons sugar (keep natural, minimally processed sugar on hand for these drinks)

Pinch of ground cinnamon

6 cups whole milk (organic)

1 cup miniature marshmallows (optional)

In a saucepan over medium-low heat, whisk together the cocoa, sugar, and cinnamon. Pour in 2 to 3 tablespoons of the milk and whisk to make a paste and begin to dissolve the sugar. Add the remaining milk and stir until well combined and hot. Pour into cups and add marshmallows, if desired. ∗

COCOA

Buy the best-quality unsweetened cocoa powder available, at least 75 percent cacao. It'll make a difference in flavor and in health benefits, and it will keep for a long time if sealed well and stored in a cool, dark place. Dutch-processed cocoa is treated to neutralize the acidity and make it taste smoother. Don't buy the "just add boiling water" hot chocolate powder, which is overly sweetened and contains dry milk.

lunch
it really matters

Plan it, pack it to go, or serve it at home,
but don't skip it. Prioritize a midday respite
for mind, body, health, and vitality and avoid an
afternoon slump.

savory chicken pocket pies

makes 10 pocket pies

One of the kids came home from school one day asking for Hot Pockets, saying he'd eaten them at a friend's house. A supermarket freezer item, Hot Pockets come two in a box, and one boy could easily gobble up two boxes in one sitting. They are processed, laden with preservatives, and expensive, and I loathe them. Still, their utility is undeniable. So I decided to re-create a similarly attractive homemade version—something the kids could quickly heat up by themselves and snack on. The idea was to replicate the convenience, but use the best ingredients according to the boys' specifications. I came up with a spinach version and a chicken one. For younger children, bake the pockets first, then cool and freeze (Step 5) so they can simply be heated up in the microwave. For older boys, freeze the pockets unbaked (Step 4); the boys can bake the pockets themselves, straight out of the freezer into the oven.

1 3-pound chicken (to get 1 heaping cup of shredded meat; you can freeze remainder for other recipes)

2 tablespoons unsalted butter

½ cup chopped onion

⅓ cup chopped celery (1 large stalk)

⅓ cup chopped carrot (1 carrot)

½ teaspoon coarse salt

2 tablespoons all-purpose flour

1½ cups chicken broth (from the reduced poaching liquid)

¼ cup grated Parmesan cheese

1 recipe (2 disks) Cream Cheese Pastry (recipe follows)

1 large egg, for egg wash

1. Place the chicken in a pot and add water to barely cover. Bring to a boil, reduce the heat, and simmer for 50 minutes. Skim and discard any foam as it rises to the surface. Remove the chicken to cool. Continue to boil the broth to reduce and concentrate to about 1 quart. Remove the meat from the chicken and shred.

2. To make the filling, melt the butter in a medium-sized hot skillet and add the onion, celery, and carrot. Sauté over medium heat for 2 to 3 minutes. Stir in the salt and flour and cook for 1 minute more. Add the chicken broth and stir until thickened, about 2 minutes. Stir in 1 heaping cup shredded chicken and the Parmesan cheese. Cool in the fridge.

3. Preheat the oven to 375°F. Butter or line a baking sheet.

4 To form the pocket pies, work with half of a disk of dough at a time, rolling it out on a floured surface. See page 65 for rolling instructions. Using an overturned bowl (about 5 inches across), cut out circles about 3 at a time from each piece of dough. After cutting out all your circles, gather all dough scraps, reroll, and cut out a final time. Place ¼ cup filling on one side of a dough circle. Wet the edges of the dough with water. Fold the dough over to form a half circle. Pinch the edges of the dough together. Crimp the edges with a fork. Repeat the process until all the filling is used. The pocket pies can be frozen at this point.

5 Place the pocket pies on the prepared baking sheet and chill for a few minutes. Prick each pie on top twice with a fork. When ready to bake, beat the egg with 1 tablespoon water. Brush the egg wash over each pocket pie. Bake for 20 to 25 minutes, until golden brown. Let rest for 5 minutes before serving. The pies can be cooled and frozen to reheat in the microwave. ⋆

Chicken Shortcut You can also use leftover shredded chicken (see page 78) and store-bought broth. Then you can start at Step 2.

Freezing and Baking Pocket Pies

Place freshly prepared pies in a single layer on a baking sheet and put in the freezer. Once they are frozen solid, they can be stacked together in a resealable bag or wrapped in plastic for easy storage. To bake from frozen, place on a baking sheet, brush with egg wash, and bake according to the recipe but for a few minutes longer.

cream cheese pastry

makes 10 pocket pies, or 1 double-crusted 10-inch pie

For a novice baker, this is the most forgiving dough to work with. The cream cheese allows this pastry some elasticity but still produces tender and flaky results. It also adds a yummy crackery flavor to the crust. Unconventionally for pie dough, the butter isn't ice-cold for this recipe.

8 tablespoons (1 stick) unsalted butter, at room temperature

4 ounces cream cheese, at room temperature

¼ cup heavy cream

1½ cups plus 2 tablespoons all-purpose flour, plus more for rolling out the dough

½ teaspoon coarse salt

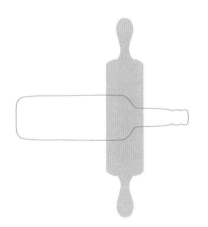

1 Process the butter, cream cheese, and cream in a food processor, electric mixer, or by hand to thoroughly combine.

2 Add the flour and salt. Process just until combined and the dough holds together in a ball. Turn the dough out onto a well-floured surface. Divide into 2 pieces. Flatten into disks and wrap each in plastic wrap. Refrigerate for at least 30 minutes before rolling out. If the dough is chilled overnight, take it out 15 minutes before rolling out.

3 Rub flour all over a rolling pin. Working with one dough disk at a time, place the disk on a clean, well-floured surface. Applying some pressure with the rolling pin, roll gently from the center of the dough to the top and bottom edges. Rotate the disk, and roll to the top and bottom edges again. Reflour the work surface and rolling pin, turn the dough over, and continue to roll the dough from the center out to the edges. Turn over and roll again, rotating the disk to ensure even rolling until the dough is about 12 inches in diameter, thin but not transparent. ✳

Yes, You Can Roll Out Dough!

Make sure you have a clean, dry, and floured surface large enough to handle the size of the dough you're rolling out—usually about 14 by 14 inches is fine. Keep an extra pile of flour nearby and lightly re-flour the surface and your rolling pin often. (Don't panic if you don't have a rolling pin; I've made many pies using a recycled wine bottle.) Be careful not to overwork this dough—unlike yeast dough for bread, which must be kneaded, pie dough should be handled as little as possible to avoid a tough, non-flaky crust.

To transport the dough to a pan, roll it onto the rolling pin (like a roll of paper towels), then unfurl it onto the pan.

spinach feta pocket pies

makes about 10 pocket pies

Just like the Savory Chicken Pocket Pies on page 62, these freeze beautifully for a quick lunch. I also serve them as a side dish to lamb as part of a larger meal. This filling can also be doubled and made into a 10-inch round pie to serve in wedges.

1 tablespoon extra-virgin olive oil

½ cup chopped onion

2 cups cooked spinach, squeezed of liquid and chopped (about 2 pounds, fresh)

½ teaspoon coarse salt

1 large egg, beaten

¼ cup crumbled feta cheese

2 tablespoons chopped fresh dill, or 1 tablespoon chopped dry dill

1 recipe (2 disks) Cream Cheese Pastry (page 65)

1 large egg, for egg wash

1 To make the filling, heat the olive oil in a medium skillet over medium heat. Add the onion, and sauté until the onion is translucent, about 3 minutes. Stir in the spinach and salt and cook to fully combine, about 2 minutes. Remove from the heat and cool slightly. Mix in the beaten egg, cheese, and dill. Chill.

2 Preheat the oven to 375°F. Butter or line a baking sheet.

3 To form the pocket pies, work with half of a disk of dough at a time, rolling it out on a floured surface. See page 65 for rolling instructions. Using an overturned bowl (about 5 inches across), cut out circles about 3 or 4 at a time from each piece of dough. After cutting circles from both disks, gather dough scraps once and reroll for the last circles. Place ¼ cup filling on one side of a dough circle. Wet the edges of the dough with water. Fold the dough over to form a half circle. Pinch the edges of the dough together. Crimp the edges with a fork. Roll out the second disk and repeat the process until all the filling is used. The pocket pies can be frozen at this point (See single layer freezing, page 63).

4 Place the pocket pies on the prepared baking sheet and chill for a few minutes. Prick each pie on top twice with a fork. When ready to bake, beat the egg with 1 tablespoon water. Brush the egg wash over each pocket pie. Bake for 20 to 25 minutes, or until golden brown. Let rest for 5 minutes before serving. The pies can be cooled and frozen to reheat in the microwave. ∗

beef empanadas

makes 10 pocket pies

Empanadas—pastry with a savory meat and vegetable filling—are a Spanish and South and Central American specialty and popular street food. At the ballfields in Riverside Park near our home in New York City, the "empanada lady" sells them during warm-weather months; we know it's summer when she shows up. After playing soccer, the boys purchase either beef or cheese empanadas for two dollars each and absolutely devour them. Hers are fried; mine are a healthier baked version. I use cream cheese pastry, which isn't authentic—but which is delicious and always easy to work with. You can make the filling up to 2 days in advance.

1 tablespoon olive oil

1 small onion, chopped

1 small green bell pepper, chopped

1 pound ground beef

1 teaspoon ground cumin

¾ cup pimiento-filled green olives, sliced

¾ cup raisins

1 teaspoon honey

1 teaspoon coarse salt

¼ teaspoon freshly ground black pepper

Several dashes of hot sauce

2 large eggs, separated

1 recipe Cream Cheese Pastry (page 65)

1 To make the filling, heat a large skillet over medium heat, and then swirl in the olive oil. Add the onion and bell pepper. Sauté until the onion is translucent, 3 to 4 minutes. Raise the heat to high and add the beef. Cook, stirring constantly, to brown, about 5 to 7 minutes. Add the cumin and cook for another minute.

2 Stir in the olives, raisins, honey, salt, pepper, and hot sauce. Cook until the meat is golden brown, the liquid has evaporated, and the flavors have blended, about 4 more minutes. Cool the mixture completely in the fridge. Stir in the egg whites.

3 Preheat the oven to 375°F degrees. Butter or line a baking sheet.

4 To form the empanadas, work with half of a disk of dough at a time, rolling out on a floured surface. Using an overturned bowl (about 5 inches across), cut out circles about 3 or 4 at a time from each piece of dough. Gather all dough scraps together, reroll once, and cut. Place ¼ cup filling on one side of a dough circle. Wet the edges of the dough with water. Fold the dough over to form a half circle. Pinch the edges of the dough together. Crimp the edges with a fork. Repeat the process until all the filling is used. The empanadas can be frozen at this point (see page 63).

5 Place the empanadas on the prepared baking sheet and chill for a few minutes. Prick each pie on top twice with a fork. When ready to bake, beat the egg yolks with 1 tablespoon water. Brush the egg wash over each empanada. Bake for 20 to 25 minutes, until golden brown. Let rest for 5 minutes before serving. The empanadas can be cooled and frozen to reheat in a microwave. ⋆

Make them bite-sized For appetizers, follow the recipe but cut each piece of dough into 3-inch rounds. Fill with 1 to 2 teaspoons of filling. Bake for 12 to 15 minutes.

Food as Medicine

"Your food should be your medicine,
and your medicine your food."

—Hippocrates (460–377 B.C.E.)

What you consume on a daily basis is your first line of defense against ill health. Be mindful with your choices. If you're suffering from a clogged head cold or excessive hay fever, eating dairy products probably isn't a good idea. But a potent, steaming-hot broth can cut through the fog of a bad cold and also deliver nutrients. Use tea to comfort or soothe. Fresh vegetables and fruits promote good health. The old axiom "An apple a day keeps the doctor away" is actually true. The fiber in apples helps keep the body's plumbing working—another key to fine health. Pay as much attention to your child's eating habits as you do to their grades. These are practical organic solutions to preventable problems.

Regularly sitting down to meals in a warm, convivial atmosphere promotes happiness and helps kids adjust to the community at large once they venture out. A healthful breakfast will provide and maintain energy. A family meal at dinnertime sustains you for the evening ahead and facilitates family communication. From the earliest possible age, open a dialogue about food—how it affects our body and makes us feel. Avoid discussions of deprivation that involve withholding the "bad" in favor of the "good." If you offer healthful "good" foods routinely, then the "bad" foods will become background players. Good food is good medicine, which assists in the treatment and prevention of disease. It doesn't take a doctor to figure this out.

My philosophy when it comes to what food I buy, consume, and serve others is I'd rather invest my dollars on best-quality food choices than on new clothes or a new car. I prefer organic produce to the conventional supermarket choices but will choose nonorganic if the vegetable is grown locally and spends less time traveling or sitting around in a warehouse. I'm concerned about taste, time spent between field and plate, and our exposure to pesticides and preservatives. The same is true for milk—I choose organic to avoid the added hormones unless the milk comes from a local, well-cared-for herd of cows that aren't given hormones—whether certified organic or not. If I have access to fresh eggs laid from happy nonorganic chickens, I buy them or otherwise seek out the next best option.

Most boys like meat. My ideal for all our sons' future is a day when they can procure meat and poultry to eat that is humanely raised—ethics, ecology, and flavor are one and the same. Restoring the balance of family farming versus factory farming is one of the most important social, political, and health issues of our time. The Farmforward site (www.farmforward.com), a "steering wheel" for this critical movement, will teach you about conscientious meat choices. Cast your vote at the supermarket checkout line with your purchasing decisions. The more we buy from companies that treat food, workers, and animals with respect, the sooner healthier, affordable choices will be available to everyone.

Meanwhile, the reality of meat and poultry choices at the grocery store is a different story. Try to buy poultry, beef, pork, and lamb labeled hormone-, antibiotic-, and cage-free even though these labels can be misleading and imperfect. I've seen raging hormones in adolescent boys, and logic tells me they don't need any more.

When it comes to fish, try to cook and eat what's available fresh, local, and of a sustainable variety (which is constantly changing). A visit to the Seafood Choices Alliance site (www.seafoodchoices.com) will give you up-to-date information about our fish supply, so you can make up your own mind. Inferior farmed varieties often have an insipid taste, bad texture, and a poor environmental track record.

While I admit to loving white bread, I will always choose to serve a nutritious whole-grain alternative at home on a daily basis. Home-baked goods are welcome, too, but store-bought choices high in processed sugar and salt are an unnecessary temptation for no good reason. So I choose to keep sugar use to a minimum at all times, especially with kids—I have learned anecdotally that everything from weight, mood, tooth hygiene, and teenage pores does better on limited sugar intake. Just watch a tired and hungry kid with a low blood-sugar level. You'll see crankiness, temper tantrums, fights, and emotional mood swings to name just a few symptoms. Frankly, the same is true of adults. The wrong food choice at the wrong time is totally counterproductive.

Yet, if organic or local food purchases are unavailable to you or prohibitive to your pocketbook, fresh-cooked conventional produce, meats, and dairy are still a smarter choice for your family's diet than inferior meals of overly processed and packaged fast food.

learn to improvise—
especially if you live with males who put empty cartons and bottles back on the shelves so you find out that you're out of something when it's too late. That's what happened last time I made this burger recipe— no ketchup, hence the use of Worcestershire sauce.

BURGER TEMPLATE

1. GROUND BEEF

When choosing ground beef for a burger, fat content is important for flavor. If possible, be mindful of where your meat comes from—in the USA, you should check the USDA rating on your meat, beholden to standards of safety and quality. Wherever you live, it's wise to buy domestically produced meat. Most everyday supermarket shoppers will use a supermarket ground chuck steak. Try combining a high-quality lean ground sirloin with a 75 percent lean ground chuck (higher in fat) for an upgraded flavor and texture. Buying it freshly ground from a butcher is even better. Aside from chuck, burger aficionados use a combination, which may include brisket, sirloin, flatiron, and skirt or hanger steak. Each cut of meat brings a different flavor and texture balance to the burger, just as different grape varietals combine to make a fine wine. One of my favorite restaurants blends a small percentage of ground lamb into the beef mix.

Time permitting, bring the meat to room temperature for about 30 minutes before cooking to help it brown instead of steam. Consider the size of the patty (thin or thick, small or large), bun choice, and cooking method (broiled, grilled, or pan-fried). Form the patty slightly larger than the bun as it will shrink when cooked. For a tender and juicy result, handle the meat as little as possible. And salt and pepper each patty aggressively just before cooking.

2. BUNS

Consider the relationship of the bun to the meat. The bun must absorb the juices while holding together enough to accommodate both burger and topping. The way you choose to prepare the bun (plain or toasted? soft but heated?) affects the outcome, too. Here are some options.

- **Martin's potato roll (my favorite)**—just firm enough to hold together but soft enough to marry well with patty and condiments. Butter and toast to a light crisp on the inside yet soft and warm on the outside.
- **English muffin**—heresy to some but heaven to others who appreciate the firm platform and those crannies, which catch juice and sauce. The extra-large version is preferable for accommodating a large patty and a hungry man.
- **Brioche roll**—buttery *and* soft.
- **Old-fashioned hamburger bun (soft)**— you have to toast, griddle, or heat for it to work well.
- **Kaiser-style roll (with or without seeds)**— deli sandwich meets burger. Some find it too hard but it makes for handy eating since it holds the add-ons well.

3. CONDIMENTS + ADD-ONS

- **Cheese**—cheddar, Muenster, Monterey Jack, Colby, provolone, American, blue, or a combination thereof. Add sliced cheese, cover with a pot lid, and let melt with 1 minute left for the burger to cook (grated needs only 30 seconds).
- **Onions**—red, white, yellow. If you want raw and slightly crunchy, a thinly sliced onion is best. If soft onions are preferred, sauté and deglaze first with vinegar or an alcohol such as bourbon, cognac, or wine.
- **Pickles, lettuce, tomato**—sliced dill pickles add an acidic flavor balance; bread and butter pickles, a sweet one. Clean, dry lettuce leaves or shredded lettuce bring a fresh crunch. Thinly slice tomatoes with a serrated knife for their soft yet cool, moist texture. Pat dry if the slices are too wet.
- **Ketchup, American yellow or Dijon mustard, mayo**—Worcestershire or barbecue sauce can stand in for ketchup. If you're out of mayo, try butter.
- **Bacon**—few men will refuse a bacon burger if it's offered. For using precooked and frozen bacon, see page 21.

4. COOKING METHOD

No matter the cooking method, if you want the burger to form a crust and retain its juicy moisture within, never move the burger until it has released from the pan's surface on its own, and never press the meat with a spatula.

- **Panfried**—probably the most common home-cooking method. Get your skillet really hot before adding your burger. The relatively cool temperature of the meat and the coating of fat in the skillet will prevent burning. Turn only once, rather than "flipping" burgers. Be careful to scrape up every brown bit. (Open a window or turn on a fan.)
- **Grilled**—start with a hot grill. Coals must be gray and very hot, otherwise the meat will steam and absorb smoke flavor before forming a crust.
- **Broiler**—flame-broiled is heralded by many a burger joint, but at home there is rarely enough flame. Broiling is less odorous than stovetop panfrying and thus is favored by some, but rarely are the results as good as panfrying. Turn on the broiler, then heat the broiling pan for several minutes before adding the meat, for best results.

burgers
makes 6 burgers

One thing is for sure: make a perfect burger, regardless of how you do it, and you make a happy man. Though there are many roads to the perfect burger, ground meat and bun are mandatory basics—condiments and improvisation determine individual style (see pages 72–73).

6 buns for hamburgers (see page 73)

1 tablespoon unsalted butter, softened

Coarse salt and freshly ground black pepper

2 pounds ground beef, formed into 6 patties

1 teaspoon Worcestershire sauce (optional)

6 slices mild cheddar cheese

½ red onion, thinly sliced (about ½ cup)

2 tablespoons mayonnaise

ketchup (optional)

mustard (optional)

3 lettuce leaves, cut in half

3 dill pickles, thinly cut horizontally

1 Preheat the broiler or preheat the oven to 400°F. Cut the buns in half and place them cut side up on a rimmed baking sheet. Spread with the butter.

2 Heat a large skillet over high heat. Generously salt and pepper the beef patties. Space the patties in the skillet without touching, and cook, without turning or flattening, for 4 to 6 minutes (depending on thickness). Turn the burgers and cook for another 4 to 6 minutes. If desired, swirl the Worcestershire into the pan 2 minutes before the burgers are finished. (Do this if you have inferior meat or no ketchup.)

3 With 1 minute left to cook, place a cheese slice on each burger. Cover with a pot lid and cook until melted. Lay onion slices on top of the melting cheese. (If using sautéed onions, place under the cheese before melting.) Remove the burgers to a plate or board to rest for a few seconds before placing them on the buns.

4 Meanwhile, broil or toast the buns for 1 to 5 minutes, until golden on the cut side and still soft on the outside.

5 Spread mayonnaise on one side of each bun. Lay a burger on top. (Top with ketchup and mustard, if using.) Garnish with lettuce and top with the other half of the bun. Serve immediately with a side of sliced dill pickles. *

italian pressed sandwiches

serves 6

Boys love Italian hero sandwiches. This pressed version borrows those flavors, but with less bread, more filling, and a compact result. Lay out sandwich fixings—your choice—on a whole loaf of bread that's been halved lengthwise, then cut it into several sections for a quick and efficient way to make multiple sandwiches. You can prepare the whole sandwich the night before and cut it into individual sandwiches in the morning. The flavors actually improve over several hours, as it sits, pressed down by a heavy object, making it a great choice for a picnic or long road trip. Generally I like to keep the fillings down to a few good ingredients so you can taste the individual flavors. Try sun-dried tomatoes and dried oregano outside of tomato season. In summer, choose fresh tomatoes and basil.

1 rectangular ciabatta or other thick-crusted bread, about 18 inches long by 5 inches wide

1½ tablespoons extra-virgin olive oil

¼ pound prosciutto, thinly sliced

¼ pound hard salami, thinly sliced

½ pound fresh mozzarella cheese, sliced

Freshly ground black pepper

⅛ teaspoon dried oregano

5 whole sun-dried tomatoes in oil, thinly sliced

1 Slice the bread horizontally and lay each half, cut side up, on a work surface. Drizzle with the olive oil. On one half, lay down the prosciutto to cover. Repeat with the salami and mozzarella. Top with the pepper, oregano, and sun-dried tomatoes. Cover with the other half of the bread.

2 Press down on the sandwich and wrap tightly in plastic wrap and then foil. Press under heavy saucepans or cans for up to overnight in the refrigerator. When ready to eat or pack, unwrap the loaf, cut into servings, and serve, or rewrap and pack. ✳

The Right Bread

Make pressed sandwiches with an Italian ciabatta or French baguette or another firm-crusted bread that can stand up to the weight of the ingredients and absorb their moisture without falling apart. Sandwiches made with firm-crusted bread can also be assembled and pressed in advance. If the loaf is too thick, scoop out some bread from the inner part; this also makes room to layer the filling. Reserve for bread crumbs.

tuna salad sandwich

makes 4 to 6 sandwiches

We started serving tuna salad on sprouted wheat or rye bread when the kids were young, and now tuna salad on any other bread just doesn't taste right.

I always put the tuna in the mixing bowl first and slowly add the onion, just to get the ratio right; too much is off-putting, but you need just enough to boost and complement the tuna flavor. Take the same care with the mayonnaise. Slowly mix it in at the end to get your own desired balance of mayo to tuna. Sometimes I make the basic mixture and divide it: plain for the kids and add-ins such as pickles or capers for the others.

2 6-ounce cans water-packed white tuna

1 large scallion (both white and green parts), finely chopped, or ¼ cup or less finely chopped or grated onion

1 celery stalk, chopped

1 tablespoon fresh lemon juice (from ½ lemon)

¼ teaspoon freshly ground back pepper

¼ teaspoon coarse salt, plus more to taste

¼ cup mayonnaise, or to taste

8 to 12 slices whole-grain or rye bread

8 to 12 lettuce leaves, washed and patted dry

OPTIONAL ADD-INS

1 to 3 dashes of Tabasco sauce

2 pickles of choice, finely chopped

1 teaspoon capers, rinsed

¼ teaspoon chopped fresh dill

1 Drain the tuna, and place it in a bowl. Break up the chunks with a fork. Add the scallion and toss together. Mix in the celery, lemon juice, pepper, and salt and any optional add-ins.

2 Little by little, mix in the mayonnaise until the desired consistency is reached. Spread the tuna salad on plain or toasted bread, topped with lettuce. ∗

TUNA MELTS

For tuna melts, omit the lettuce. Toast 8 to 12 slices of bread. Top the toast with tuna salad and top with 1 slice of cheddar, Swiss, or white American cheese. Broil in a toaster oven or broiler for 3 minutes, or until the cheese is melted.

Mayonnaise versus Salad Dressing Spread Because I grew up in a Miracle Whip (salad dressing) house as opposed to a Hellmann's Mayonnaise house, it took me a while to figure out why most tuna salad never tasted like Mom's. While I successfully converted to mayonnaise through marriage, I still have to flavor it up a bit to satisfy my taste in most sandwiches.
● Hellmann's Mayonnaise—closest to homemade and includes egg yolks. Flavor neutral.
● Kraft's Miracle Whip salad dressing spread—sweeter and tarter and full of corn syrup and stabilizers—but a favored choice in some households. Fewer, if any, egg yolks.

chicken salad sandwich

makes 6 servings for sandwiches or salad

Leftover chicken, and the cooked meat used for chicken stock, are perfect for chicken salad. Here's a straightforward rendition of the classic, without a fancy or modern twist in sight. It's a traditional chicken salad that can be spread on wholesome bread and topped with a piece of crunchy lettuce (for the guys) or scooped over washed greens or stuffed in a tomato or an avocado (for the girls). For two meals from one bird, make the Chicken and Dumplings (page 125), which produces enough meat for this recipe, too.

2 cups chopped or shredded cooked chicken

½ cup chopped celery

1 tablespoon chopped fresh parsley leaves

½ teaspoon coarse salt

¼ teaspoon freshly ground black pepper

1 tablespoon fresh lemon juice

⅓ cup mayonnaise, or to taste

3 teaspoons unsalted butter, softened

12 slices whole-grain bread

6 romaine lettuce leaves, cleaned, patted dry, and chilled

1 In a medium bowl, stir together the chicken, celery, parsley, salt, pepper, and lemon juice. Stir in the mayonnaise, little by little, to achieve the desired consistency. The chicken salad can be kept, refrigerated, for 1 day.

2 Spread butter on each slice of bread. Sandwich with chicken salad and a leaf of lettuce. Serve with salty potato chips. *

EXTRA PROTECTION FOR THE BREAD

My mom always buttered the bread for our sandwiches, which used to annoy me when I was a kid. As a mother myself now, I understand the utilitarian purpose. A layer of butter protects the bread by creating a barrier between wet filling and dry bread, preventing the sandwich from going soggy and giving it a longer life. It also tastes good!

chicken soup and rice

serves 4

This is a really quick version of chicken soup made to mimic a traditional long-simmered soup. Time permitting, the latter is better. But, with a few basic pantry items, you can prepare this version in about 10 minutes. Served with salad and toast it also makes a great lunch. For times like this it's useful to keep small packets of cooked chicken breast and rice upfront in the freezer.

1 tablespoon olive oil

1 tablespoon unsalted butter

3 scallions (both white and green parts), thinly sliced

1 large carrot, peeled and chopped

½ cup chopped fresh parsley leaves

1 quart (4 cups) homemade chicken broth (see below) or best-quality store-bought chicken broth

1 cup cooked, shredded chicken meat (leftover or 1 chicken breast half, sautéed or steamed)

½ cup cooked rice

Coarse salt and freshly ground black pepper

1 Heat a medium-sized soup pot over medium heat and swirl in the olive oil and butter. Sauté the scallions, carrot, and parsley for 2 to 3 minutes. Add the chicken broth and simmer until the carrot is cooked through, about 5 minutes.

2 Add the chicken and rice. Heat through completely, about 3 minutes. Taste and season with salt and pepper. Serve immediately. ∗

Another Quick Method for Cooking Chicken Preheat the oven to 400°F. Line a rimmed baking sheet with foil or baking parchment. Place 4 to 6 boneless, skinless chicken breasts on the sheet. Sprinkle with olive oil, salt, and pepper and top loosely with a sheet of parchment. Bake until just cooked through, about 15 to 20 minutes, turning once. Cool and use as needed; freeze leftovers. A breast half makes 1 to 1½ cups of shredded chicken.

Homemade Chicken Broth Don't be intimidated by homemade chicken broth. It can be as simple or as complicated as you have time for. Cover chicken bones or parts with water, bring to a boil, simmer for 30 minutes, add salt (or not), skim, and you have an enriched liquid to cook with that is better than any commercial canned broth. Time permitting, you can slowly simmer a chicken with water, vegetables, herbs, and spices, strain, and simmer some more to concentrate the flavor. Easily stored in the freezer for soups, stews, or sauces, it's well worth the time spent making it. Best-quality boxed or canned chicken broth, available everywhere, can also be used, but so far no commercial manufacturer has made a product for mass consumption that comes close to homemade in flavor.

chicken broth elixir

makes 1 quart

When the college semester ends, sleep-deprived twenty-year-olds arrive home depleted and often sick. As our boys know, my first line of defense is always a natural one. My college-age son, who recently brought home the worst kind of early-summer head cold, learned this as a five-year-old when his whooping cough finally waned after a daily course of four cups of mullein tea with honey. For years after that he wouldn't drink tea, but now he's the first to cooperate with our homemade healing concoctions. When the requisite natural remedies—tea with lemon, herbal Echinacea tincture, and Emergen-C (a flavored fizzy energy booster with 1,000 milligrams of vitamin C)—fail to work quickly, I move to Plan B: sleep, coupled with this steaming hot broth four times throughout the day to drive impurities out of the body fast. Garlic has antibiotic properties, onions expectorant ones, and chilies and ginger cut through the fog and deliver vitamin C. These flu fighters, suspended in a protein-concentrated broth, make good medicine! My prescription? Drink a mugful as hot as you can tolerate. Go to bed, pull up cozy covers, sleep, and repeat. It gently restores strength and cleans out toxins as you sweat. I nursed my dad and several boys back from the brink of sickness with this broth.

2 chicken backs, necks, and wing tips, cut from whole chickens used for other recipes	Place all ingredients in a stockpot and barely cover with water. Bring to a boil, reduce the heat, and simmer, partially covered, for 1 hour. Skim and discard any foam as it rises to the surface. Strain the broth. (The cooked chicken meat can be used for chicken salad; see page 78.) Return the broth to the heat and simmer to reduce it to 1½ quarts. To store, place in plastic freezable containers, cool, and seal. *
6 chicken thighs	
1 large yellow onion, quartered	
4 garlic cloves, smashed	
2 celery stalks, coarsely chopped	
1 tablespoon coarse salt	

FOR AN ASIAN FLAVOR

To add even more nutrients or in recipes with an Asian theme, add 3 inches of washed and sliced ginger and 2 spicy chili peppers. Then strain with the other ingredients.

meaty noodle soup, asian style

serves 4 to 6

This is another nourishing soup, and a favorite of the boys I know, all of whom seem to love to chew and slurp on the noodles in all manner of delivery systems. It's not a quick soup, though, as it needs some time to develop its deep flavor, but it's a delicious and satisfying soup for any meal.

3 pounds short ribs or beef shanks

1 pound pork chops

10 cups water

1 onion, halved

3 garlic cloves, smashed

2 inches of peeled fresh ginger, 1 inch sliced, the rest minced

1 bay leaf

2 whole star anise

2 bird or serrano chilies

10 peppercorns

3 tablespoons soy sauce or tamari

4 dry shiitake mushrooms

4 pieces of dried kelp (optional)

2 scallions (both white and green parts), finely sliced

1 shallot, peeled and finely sliced

2 teaspoons coarse salt, plus more to taste

1 cup shredded napa cabbage, bok choy, or spinach

½ pound soba (or other Asian noodles [see page 84])

½ teaspoon toasted sesame oil or vegetable oil

Chili paste, for serving

1 Place the beef, pork, and water into a large stockpot. Add the onion, garlic, sliced ginger, bay leaf, 1 star anise, whole chilies, peppercorns, soy sauce, mushrooms, and kelp, if using. Bring to a boil, reduce the heat, and simmer for 2 hours, partially covered. Skim and discard any foam as it rises to the surface.

2 Strain the broth through a cheesecloth-lined sieve. Remove the meat from the bones and shred. Discard the bones. Return the broth to gently boil for 15 minutes.

3 Add the scallions, minced ginger, shallot, salt, and remaining star anise to the broth. Stir in the reserved meat and the cabbage.

4 Meanwhile, bring a large pot of water to a boil, add the noodles, and cook until just tender, 3 to 4 minutes, or according to the package instructions. Drain well. Toss them with the sesame oil to coat.

5 Place a nest of noodles in each bowl, ladle the soup over the top, and serve with chili paste on the side. ∗

PEELING GINGER

To peel ginger, scrape the skin of the root with the inside of a teaspoon, digging the edge of the spoon into the crevices of the gingerroot. You can use a paring knife or vegetable peeler, but more ginger is lost in peeling than when using a spoon.

oxtail broth with noodles

serves 4 to 6

Oxtails make exceptional earthy, beef-flavored soup broths, especially if simmered long enough to become very soft and melted. Oxtail used to be an incredibly economical purchase until it became fashionable at high-end restaurants. In many large ethnic markets it's still a bargain, especially the smaller quantity needed for a soup base rather than a main dish. No complicated cooking methods necessary—all that's required is simmering time—to make it soft and melting. Pour the hot broth over the oxtails and fill the bowl up with a nest of cooked noodles—grab and cook whichever ones you have in the cupboard, such as udon. Serve the dipping sauce on the side.

2 to 3 pounds oxtails

6 garlic cloves, smashed

4 whole scallions, crushed

10 cups water

1 teaspoon coarse salt

8 ounces noodles, preferably udon

DIPPING SAUCE

½ cup soy sauce

1 teaspoon rice vinegar

½ teaspoon toasted sesame oil

2 teaspoons sugar

1 scallion (both white and green parts), thinly sliced

1 hot green chili, thinly sliced

2 tablespoons water

1 Place the oxtails, garlic, 3 of the scallions, and the water into a large pot. Bring to a boil over high heat; reduce the heat and simmer, partially covered, for 3 hours. Skim and discard any foam as it rises to the surface. Discard the garlic and scallions. Stir in the salt.

2 Bring a large pot of water to a boil over high heat, add the noodles, and cook until just tender, about 5 minutes, or according to the package instructions.

3 Meanwhile, combine the ingredients for the dipping sauce and divide among small individual bowls.

4 Drain the noodles, rinse, and toss with a small amount of the oxtail broth. Place an oxtail and some noodles in each serving bowl. Ladle over the hot broth. Serve with the small bowls of dipping sauce on the side. *

STEAL IDEAS FROM THEIR FRIENDS

Sometimes your kids will eat foods at their friends' houses that you can't imagine them eating at home. A meat-eating boy, while caught up in his buddy's family experience, might be unwittingly lulled into trying sautéed kale, a vegetable curry, or baked fish—foods he thinks he hates. And if you serve some unusual dishes in your own home, your children's friends will likely try something they might not eat in their home.

malaysian-style chicken and shrimp laksa

serves 4

For several weeks, my middle son bugged me to make laksa, a popular spicy noodle soup with Chinese and Malay elements popular in Malaysia and Singapore. It can be prepared in several different styles, but they all include noodles and spicy sauce. I did some research, used a little intuition, and released myself from the angst of getting all the "perfect" ingredients.

CHILI PASTE

6 long dried red chilies, stemmed (use a few more for blazing heat)

6 shallots, average size, peeled and coarsely chopped

2 to 3 inches of fresh galangal or ginger, peeled and coarsely chopped

2 lemongrass stalks, tough dark green stems removed, coarsely chopped

2 tablespoons peanut oil (or favorite vegetable oil, not olive)

½ teaspoon ground turmeric (if you can get fresh, use more)

2 tablespoons fish sauce, or 1 teaspoon shrimp paste

1 garlic clove, coarsely chopped

¼ cup water

LAKSA

½ pound large shrimp with shells on

3 cups best-quality chicken broth

8 ounces favorite noodles, such as rice noodles or lo mein

1½ tablespoons peanut oil

2 boneless skinless chicken breasts (1 pound)

Coarse salt and freshly ground black pepper

1 cup reserved chili paste

1 14-ounce can coconut milk

5 to 6 ounces fresh bean sprouts

1 cup fresh mint leaves, loosely packed

2 shallots, sliced thin and fried in oil (optional)

¼ cup best-quality sambal chili sauce, for garnish (optional)

THE MISSING INGREDIENT

Don't be paralyzed if the market doesn't have that one unusual ingredient the recipe calls for. Either leave it out or be creative in finding a substitute. If substituting, think about the role that the ingredient plays in the final dish. If I can't find galangal (a root with a gingery, peppery flavor), I use fresh ginger; if I can't find shrimp paste, I choose fish sauce or anchovy paste. No Vietnamese-style mint? Try regular mint. Any hot pepper sauce can give you the spicy heat of sambal chili sauce.

1 Peel the shrimp and place the shells in a small saucepan along with the chicken broth (refrigerate the shrimp until needed in step 5). Bring the broth to a boil and reduce the heat to gently simmer for 15 minutes. Drain the broth and reserve. Discard the shells.

2 Meanwhile, make the chili paste: Soak the red chilies in boiling water for 5 minutes; drain. Place the drained chilies and the remaining chili paste ingredients in a food processor or blender. Blend to a smooth paste and set aside.

3 Bring a large pot of water to a boil over high heat, add the noodles, and cook until just tender, about 5 minutes, or according to the package instructions. Drain well. Lightly toss them with 1½ teaspoon of the oil to avoid sticking together, and set aside. Reheat the noodles for 40 seconds in a microwave before serving.

4 Meanwhile, season the chicken breasts with salt and pepper on both sides. Place the pot used for the noodles over medium-high heat. Swirl the remaining tablespoon of oil around the bottom of the pan. Sear the breasts for 5 minutes per side, or until just done. Remove from the pot. Let the chicken cool, then slice thin.

5 While the chicken is cooling, add the reserved 1 cup of chili paste to the hot pan and sauté for 2 minutes. Stir in the coconut milk and the reserved shrimp-chicken broth. Bring to a boil, reduce to a simmer, and let the sauce reduce for 5 minutes. Stir in the shrimp. After 1 minute, stir in the sliced chicken. Cook for another minute, until the shrimp is opaque and everything is completely heated through.

6 In each bowl, place a mound of noodles and spoon the hot laksa mixture over the noodles for a soupy consistency. Divide the shrimp and chicken among the bowls. Garnish with bean sprouts and mint to taste. Sprinkle on the fried shallots, if using. Serve immediately. Place a small bowl of extra chili sauce on the table, if desired. ∗

Asian Soup Noodles All manner of Asian noodles can be easily gussied up with a few pantry ingredients such as sesame oil or soy or hot sauce. Drain cooked noodles right away so they don't clump together. After draining, lightly coat the noodles with sesame or vegetable oil. Unless you live near specialty stores or order online, you'll probably be shopping at the supermarket. These are usually readily available:

- **Egg or wheat noodles:** both the thin and thick versions. Boil for 3 to 5 minutes, depending on the size, until just tender.
- **Soba:** buckwheat and brown noodles. Boil for 2 to 4 minutes, drain, and coat.
- **Udon:** thick wheat noodles, heavy and chewy. Boil for about 6 minutes.
- **Cellophane noodles or rice sticks:** soak to soften and drain before dressing or adding to soup broth.
- **Spaghetti:** use in a pinch where noodles are called for in Asian dishes.

lentil vegetable soup

serves 6 to 8

For heartiness and economy, you can't beat this soup for feeding boys. Even the pricey organic French lentils cost only about four dollars for the 2 cups needed. And, unlike other long-simmering soups, this one cooks in under an hour. I like to keep this meatless, but you can easily sauté bacon or pancetta with the onions. Make it on a Saturday morning and keep it on the stove for everyone to eat on his or her own time throughout the day. Refrigerate for the next day's lunch, too. Or, prepare it on a Sunday for Monday dinner—the flavor will only improve. Make a big batch of croutons to top it off, another "fill-up-the-stomach" technique for hungry males. For an entirely vegetarian version, use vegetable broth.

2½ tablespoons extra-virgin olive oil

1 onion, chopped (¾ cup)

2 carrots, peeled and chopped (¾ cup)

2 celery stalks, peeled and chopped (⅔ cup)

3 garlic cloves, minced (1 tablespoon)

1 tablespoon coarse salt

1 small tomato, chopped (⅓ cup)

1 tablespoon tomato paste

2 cups brown or green lentils

½ teaspoon dried thyme

1 small bay leaf

¼ teaspoon freshly ground black pepper

6 cups chicken broth or vegetable broth

4 cups water, plus more if needed

2 teaspoons red wine vinegar

CROUTONS (OPTIONAL)

½ loaf day-old bread

3 tablespoons extra-virgin olive oil

2 garlic cloves, crushed

¼ teaspoon coarse salt

1 Heat a large soup pot over high heat and swirl in the olive oil. Add the onion, carrots, celery, garlic, and 1 teaspoon of the salt. Reduce the heat to low and sauté until the vegetables are lightly caramelized, about 5 minutes. Add the tomato and cook for 2 minutes. Stir in the tomato paste and cook for another 2 minutes.

2 Add the lentils, thyme, bay leaf, pepper, and the remaining 2 teaspoons salt. Add the broth and water, and bring to a boil, skimming and discarding any foam as it rises to the surface. Reduce the heat and simmer until the lentils are tender, 15 to 20 minutes. (The cooking time depends on the age of the dried lentils.) Stir in the vinegar. Season to taste with salt and pepper. If needed, thin the soup with additional water or broth for the desired consistency. Serve in a bowl topped with the fresh croutons, if using.

3 To make the croutons, cut the bread into ¾-inch cubes. Heat a large skillet over high heat and add the olive oil, swirling to coat the bottom of the pan. Add the garlic and cook until it sizzles, about 50 seconds. Add the bread and cook, stirring, until golden brown, about 2 minutes. Discard the garlic. Sprinkle the croutons with the salt and serve over the soup. ∗

boy salads

Boys will eat salads, but only the right salads. Some girls will eat any salads just because they think they should, but many boys will eat them only if the salads look and taste good. First and foremost, know that wet lettuce ripped into big chunks is a turnoff. But a salad prepared from cold, dry, crisp, bite-sized lettuce, mixed with carefully considered add-ins and dressed in a vibrant, acidic vinaigrette, is easy to love, especially after repeat exposure. Washed and dried lettuce is the key to a great salad.

Washing, Drying, and Storing Greens

Romaine is sturdy yet leafy and makes a good choice for boy salads. Boston, also known as Bibb lettuce, is good in combination with other greens but very tender on its own. Trim off the outer leaves. Fill a giant bowl with ice-cold water and float the leaves in the water, swirling around gently to allow sand and soil to sink to the bottom of the bowl. Place the leaves in a colander and repeat with fresh water until all the lettuce is free of soil and sand.

To dry, place lettuce leaves evenly in a single layer, slightly overlapping, on a clean kitchen towel. Layer with a paper towel or another cloth towel until all the lettuce is stacked. If storing, roll up loosely and place the bundle into a large plastic bag—old grocery and produce bags work well—and refrigerate. It will store well for up to a week. If using a salad spinner to dry greens, don't stuff it full and expect favorable results. Work in batches. Roll the dried leaves and store as described above.

The same process applies to all greens, including spinach, kale, and chard, and especially to home-grown greens or those purchased at a farmers' market, which are often grittier and more likely to have clumps of soil adhering to them.

Cooked greens such as spinach, Swiss chard, or kale are a slightly different matter. I leave some water on the greens after the last water bath—all that is needed for them to steam on their own without added water. Be careful, though: cooking in too much water results in a mushy, watery mess. If you're storing these greens for future use, follow the drying process outlined above for lettuce.

tabbouleh salad

serves 6 as a sidedish or sandwich filling

Loaded with an abundance of parsley, bulgur wheat, mint, lemon, cucumbers, and tomatoes, this salad is a health bonanza. A complex array of irresistible textures and flavors makes it a refreshing warm-weather salad, a wonderful side dish for a roast lamb dinner, or as a part of *mezze,* an assortment of small appetizers. It also keeps well in the refrigerator for a few days, allowing the flavors to meld, making it a great do-ahead salad for both an entertaining menu and the lunch pail. You can also use it as a filling for sandwiches, layered into pita bread and topped with cold sliced lamb and some sliced feta cheese (opposite).

½ cup bulgur wheat

2 tomatoes, diced (1½ cups)

3 scallions (both white and green parts), trimmed and thinly sliced (1 cup)

2 to 3 cups chopped fresh curly parsley, stems removed

1 cucumber, peeled and diced (1 cup)

½ cup fresh mint leaves, chopped

¼ teaspoon freshly grated lemon zest

2 tablespoons fresh lemon juice

⅓ cup extra-virgin olive oil

¼ teaspoon coarse salt, or more to taste

1. Rinse the bulgur wheat in cold running water and soak in a bowl of cold water for 20 minutes. Drain and place in a large bowl.

2. Add the tomatoes, scallions, parsley, cucumber, and mint. Toss together.

3. Whisk together the lemon zest and juice, olive oil, and salt. Stir the dressing into the salad to fully combine. Serve or cover and refrigerate for up to 2 days. *

PARSLEY

This ubiquitous herb—both curly and flat-leaf Italian varieties available in abundant, affordable bunches—is one of the most underrated of herbs. It has a clean, yet mildly peppery, flavor and contains three times more vitamin C than oranges. Eating parsley leaves neutralizes the odor of garlic on the breath, and chopping parsley neutralizes a garlic odor on your cutting board. Rather than using parsley to just garnish or dust over food, try adding leaves to a basic green salad or offering a salad totally dominated by this nutritional powerhouse.

pantry bistro salad

serves 4

When you think there is no food in the house, you can prepare this satisfying and hearty salad by scrounging the fridge and pantry for a few simple ingredients. This is a facsimile of a French-style bistro salad complete with bacon and eggs, an unerring choice for the guys.

2 tablespoons extra-virgin olive oil

½ pound bacon, cut into ½-inch pieces

½ white onion, chopped

4 large eggs

2 heads of romaine lettuce, washed, dried, and chilled

2 capfuls red wine vinegar

Coarse salt and freshly ground black pepper

Toasted bread slices, for serving

1 Heat a medium skillet over medium high heat, and then swirl in 1 tablespoon of the olive oil. Add the bacon and onion and sauté until the bacon is crisp, 5 to 8 minutes. Remove the bacon and onion mixture with a slotted spoon to drain on paper towels.

2 Meanwhile, poach the eggs in gently boiling water for 2 to 3 minutes, until the white is set and the yolk is still runny. Using a slotted spoon, remove the eggs and place on a clean kitchen towel to drain.

3 Slice the lettuce into ½-inch pieces and place in a large salad bowl. Drizzle with the remaining 1 tablespoon olive oil and the vinegar and season with salt and pepper. Toss to coat the leaves.

4 Divide the lettuce among 4 bowls. Sprinkle each with the bacon mixture. Place an egg on top of each and serve immediately with toasted bread. ∗

spinach oshitashi style

serves 6

This recipe is a home-style rendition of the Japanese cold spinach appetizer, and it's a good place to start if you're trying to entice a picky kid to eat spinach. Steam the spinach, squeeze out the moisture, dress up with friendly and familiar flavors, and chill. It's great as an accompaniment to any Asian dish, as a quick lunch or snack, or as a make-ahead component of any meal with Asian flavors. Use the freshest spinach, and make sure to thoroughly wash it to remove all the grit.

2 bunches of spinach, ends trimmed, washed, with water still clinging to the leaves

1 tablespoon tamari or soy sauce

¼ teaspoon toasted sesame oil

Pinch of sugar

Dash of white wine vinegar

1 teaspoon toasted sesame seeds (optional)

1 Place the spinach in a large pot with a tight-fitting lid over high heat. Watching it carefully, steam it until the spinach has fully wilted, 3 to 4 minutes. Drain in a colander and press out the excess moisture.

2 In a small bowl, whisk together the tamari, sesame oil, sugar, and vinegar. Toss with the spinach until fully coated. Press the spinach into a shallow serving dish. Sprinkle with the sesame seeds, if desired. Cover and chill. *

tomato, avocado, and basil salad

serves 6

This simple warm-weather lunch salad easily turns into a superb vegetarian sandwich. It also makes an excellent side with anything barbecued.

6 small tomatoes, cored and cut in eighths

1 small white onion, thinly sliced

Coarse salt and freshly ground black pepper

1½ tablespoons extra-virgin olive oil

2 teaspoons mild vinegar, such as champagne vinegar or white wine vinegar

2 ripe avocados, peeled, pitted, and sliced lengthwise

¾ cup fresh basil or cilantro leaves

In a small bowl, gently toss the tomatoes and onion with salt, pepper, the olive oil, and the vinegar. Lift the vegetables out and spread on a serving platter. Lay the avocado slices on top and pour the tomato-vinegar juices onto the avocados. Scatter with the fresh basil leaves. ⁎

TO EASILY PIT AN AVOCADO

Slice lengthwise all around the avocado. Using both hands, carefully twist it apart into two pieces. Tap a knife blade into the pit and gently wiggle. The pit will come free, attached to the blade.

rose's vinaigrette

makes 1 cup

All the green salads we had while growing up were dressed with my mom's vinaigrette. My dad thought it was the best dressing there ever was. Make it directly in a jar with a tight-fitting lid and store it in the refrigerator for up to 6 months. This dressing is also key to the success of Rose's beloved White Bean Salad (page 100).

1 tablespoon minced shallot or garlic

1 teaspoon Dijon mustard

1 teaspoon light brown sugar

¾ teaspoon coarse salt

¼ teaspoon freshly ground black pepper

¼ teaspoon Worcestershire sauce

2½ tablespoons red wine vinegar

2 tablespoons fresh lemon juice

¾ cup extra-virgin olive oil

1 In the bottom of a clean jar, mash together the shallot, mustard, brown sugar, salt, pepper, and Worcestershire sauce.

2 Pour in the vinegar, lemon juice, and olive oil. Cover tightly and shake well to combine and emulsify. Add salt and pepper to taste. Use immediately or store in the refrigerator. ★

green goddess ranch salad dressing

makes 1½ cups

A creamy homemade salad dressing, free of commercial stabilizers, is another boon for salad makers. The anchovy in this one is undetectable but adds a salty, briny flavor; you can substitute salt if you're afraid you'll be found out for it. Choose your greens wisely, cleaning them thoroughly and serving them well chilled.

2 tablespoons minced fresh chives and/or scallions

2 teaspoons anchovy paste, or 1 teaspoon coarse salt

⅛ teaspoon freshly ground black pepper

½ cup sour cream

1 cup mayonnaise

2 tablespoons mild vinegar, such as white wine vinegar or tarragon vinegar

1 tablespoon fresh lemon juice

1 small garlic clove, smashed and minced

Buttermilk or milk (optional)

In a large bowl or blender, whisk or blend all the ingredients except the buttermilk. Add just enough buttermilk to thin to the desired consistency, if needed. Pour into a jar with a tight-fitting lid and refrigerate for a few hours to allow the flavors to combine. Shake well before using. Keeps in the refrigerator for up to 1 week. *

Dressing When You Don't Want to Make Dressing

Just before serving, generously drizzle extra-virgin olive oil over the salad. Add a capful or two of vinegar or a few teaspoons of tart citrus juice, depending on how acidic you like it. Distribute a large pinch of coarse salt and grind lots of black pepper over all. Toss together to completely cover the leaves, and serve.

tangy sweet salmon and rice salad

serves 6 as a side dish

I discovered two ways to get guys to eat fish: by making it part of a bigger meal that includes other offerings (meat) and mixing it with other flavorful ingredients, as in this recipe. Sooner or later they'll accept it, like it, and even ask for it for dinner. I use the procedure below for steaming a pound or more of salmon, but you can also place it in a roasting pan in a 350°F oven for about 10 minutes.

The appeal of this recipe is the unbeatable flavor combination created by toasted pine nuts, golden raisins, and fresh mint. Mixed with cold rice and flaked Copper River sockeye salmon, it makes a sublime picnic dish or hot-weather side dish. In a pinch, canned Alaskan salmon can stand in for the fresh.

1 cup jasmine or basmati rice

Coarse salt

5 scallions, 1 whole and 4 finely chopped

¼ cup chopped fresh parsley leaves

¼ teaspoon peppercorns

½ pound fresh wild salmon

¼ cup pine nuts, lightly toasted

¼ cup golden raisins

1 tablespoon freshly grated lime zest

2 tablespoons fresh lime juice

3 tablespoons extra-virgin olive oil

Freshly ground black pepper

½ cup fresh mint leaves, cut in fine strips

MAKING THE FISH APPEALING
When serving fish to boys, make sure to remove all the icky parts: dark meat, bones, skin, and gelatin. Keep the fish as clean as possible to *hook* your kids.

1 Place the rice in a pot with 1½ cups water and ½ teaspoon salt. Bring to a boil over high heat, cover, and reduce the heat to a simmer for 20 minutes, or until the rice has absorbed all the liquid. Spread out the cooked rice on a rimmed baking sheet and chill.

2 Meanwhile, in a shallow sauté pan, place 1 cup water, the whole scallion, parsley, and peppercorns and bring to a simmer. Sprinkle the fish with salt and place in the pan. Cover and poach for 5 to 9 minutes, until just cooked through. Remove the salmon and peel off and discard the skin while still hot. Chill the salmon.

3 Place the pine nuts, raisins, chopped scallions, lime zest and juice, and olive oil into a large bowl, season with salt and freshly ground black pepper, and toss to combine. Flake the salmon into the bowl and add the rice. Stir to combine. Let sit for a short while to allow the flavors to blend. You can prepare the salad 6 to 8 hours ahead of eating. If made ahead, refrigerate until ready to serve. Garnish with mint. ∗

white bean salad

serves 6 to 8

Lunch, snack, or side dish—once you make a batch of this salad, you'll find yourself using it for many different meals. If it's made in advance, the taste only improves. This is my mom's recipe. Her sons and grandsons love it. Depending on what type of meal it's planned for, she'll vary the herbs to best accent it—adding mint if served with lamb, dill with fish, basil with roast chicken. Piled on top of arugula or watercress, it's a great addition to any summer spread, and one of my favorite lunches.

3 15-ounce cans cannellini beans, drained

½ cup chopped red onion

½ cup chopped fresh parsley leaves

¼ cup chopped or torn fresh dill, mint, or basil (optional)

½ teaspoon coarse salt

¼ teaspoon freshly ground black pepper

1 recipe Rose's Vinaigrette (page 96)

3 scallions (green part only), finely sliced

1 Combine the beans in a large bowl with the red onion, parsley, optional herb of choice, salt, and pepper.

2 Slowly stir in the dressing to taste. Garnish with the scallions. Serve immediately or refrigerate. The salad will keep in the fridge for up to 3 days. *

Beans: Protein Alternative to Meat

Chickpeas, red beans, or black beans with rice and lentil and bean soups are all healthy and satisfying protein alternatives to meat and help stretch the weekly food budget. As food activist Michael Pollan suggests, "if all Americans had one meatless day per week, the reduced carbon footprint equals taking twenty million midsize sedans off the road for a year." Less meat consumed means fewer precious resources compromised in the pursuit of commercially raised livestock used for mass consumption. Reducing the amount of meat eaten also lowers your fat and cholesterol intake.

chinese celery salad

serves 4 to 6

Here celery stars in its own salad with winning results. I learned this recipe from Angel, a Cantonese Chinese home cook who served it with Cold Sesame Noodles (page 104) for lunch. Try it with Stir-Fried Chinese Chicken and Peanuts (page 130) for dinner.

1 bunch of celery, top and bottom removed, stalks separated and cut in half lengthwise

1 tablespoon rice vinegar or white vinegar

1 teaspoon toasted sesame oil

4 tablespoons soy sauce

2 dashes Chinese chili oil or hot sauce (optional)

½ teaspoon sugar

2 tablespoons chopped fresh cilantro (optional)

1 Bring a large pot of water to a boil. Add the celery and blanch for 2 minutes. Remove, rinse, and cool. Peel off the fibrous strings. Cut the celery into bite-sized pieces.

2 In a bowl, whisk together the vinegar, sesame oil, soy sauce, chili oil, if using, sugar, and cilantro, if using. Toss in the celery. Cover and refrigerate to cool before serving. ∗

cold sesame noodles

serves 4 to 6

With the possible exception of pan-fried dumplings, cold sesame noodles are probably the Chinese takeout item most frequently ordered by kids. This dish can be as quick a meal as spaghetti. A well-stocked pantry (see page 8) contains all the ingredients.

1 pound Chinese egg noodles, or spaghetti or linguine

½ teaspoon toasted sesame oil

6 tablespoons sesame paste (tahini) or peanut butter

¾ cup water, plus more if needed

1 tablespoon rice vinegar or white vinegar

3 tablespoons soy sauce

1½ teaspoons sugar

2 garlic cloves, minced

1 scallion (both white and green parts), thinly sliced

1½ inches of fresh ginger, peeled and chopped (1 tablespoon)

Chinese chili oil (optional)

1 Bring a large pot of water to a boil, add the noodles, and cook until just barely tender, 5 to 6 minutes, or according to the package instructions. Drain well. Toss them with the sesame oil to coat. Cover and refrigerate.

2 Meanwhile, in a large bowl, thin the sesame paste by stirring enough water into the paste to achieve the consistency of thick cream. Whisk together the vinegar, soy sauce, and sugar. Add the mixture to the sesame paste. Stir in the garlic, three quarters of the scallion, and the ginger.

3 Just before serving, toss the chilled noodles with the sauce. Garnish with the remaining scallion and drizzle with the chili oil, if using. ∗

Frozen dumplings

Commercially made frozen dumplings are available at many specialty food chains and markets in Chinatown communities. You can easily and quickly boil, steam, or panfry them, and they make a quick soup with some chicken broth.

potsticker dumplings
makes 36 dumplings

Like most things wrapped in dough, this is a friendly, go-to choice. The variations on dumpling fillings and shape are endless, and it is surprising how easy these are to make at home. Start with a large batch, freeze it, and you'll always have a quick snack, appetizer, or meal ready in about 8 minutes. Dumpling wrappers—Chinese wonton or Japanese gyoza skins are the same thing—are now widely available in the produce or frozen food section of most markets. I once made the filling from ground meat I found in the freezer; I defrosted it, then mixed it with some lone scallions and ginger found in the back of the crisper. "You know that's turkey, right?" my husband asked. I had thought it was pork. So, I just boosted the seasoning a little to make up for the fat flavor lacking in turkey. I made enough to eat right away and also to freeze for later.

SOY-VINEGAR DIPPING SAUCE

½ cup soy sauce

1 teaspoon rice vinegar

½ teaspoon toasted sesame oil

2 teaspoons sugar

1 whole scallion, trimmed and sliced

1 hot green chili, thinly sliced

2 tablespoons water

DUMPLINGS

½ pound ground turkey, chicken, or pork (if using poultry, add 1 teaspoon peanut oil to the mixture)

1 cup finely chopped bok choy

½ teaspoon minced peeled fresh ginger

1 small garlic clove, minced

1 teaspoon soy sauce

½ teaspoon sesame oil

½ teaspoon coarse salt

1 large egg white

36 dumpling wrappers

Peanut oil, for frying

1 In a small bowl, combine all ingredients for the dipping sauce. Set aside.

2 In a medium bowl, mix together the turkey, bok choy, ginger, garlic, soy sauce, sesame oil, and salt. Stir in the egg white.

3 Working with 6 at a time, lay down the dumpling wrappers on a work surface. Spoon 1 teaspoon of filling onto each one. Lightly wet the edge of each wrapper with water. Fold the dough over and pinch around the edges. This is easiest done by picking up each dumpling and pinching around the edges with thumb and forefinger. Place on a baking sheet and cover with plastic wrap to keep the dumplings from drying out. Repeat until all filling is used. (Freeze any dumplings that will not be cooked immediately. After they are frozen, transfer them to resealable plastic bags or wrap in plastic.)

4 To cook the dumplings, heat a large skillet and swirl some oil around to coat the pan. Add a single layer of potstickers. Cook for 2 to 3 minutes (2 minutes longer if frozen), until they begin to turn golden on the underside. Don't move them. Add ¼ cup of water to the pan and cover immediately. Cook for 5 more minutes, or until the meat is cooked through and the dumplings release from the pan. Serve immediately with the dipping sauce. ∗

cannelloni crepes

makes 12 crepes; serves 4 to 6

This great everyday dish can also feel right at home at a fancier meal. Crepes can be made ahead and kept in the refrigerator for 2 or 3 days or frozen. The whole dish can be assembled and frozen. Keep a tray of them in the freezer to feed a crowd for lunch or even as an appetizer before dinner. Bake directly from the freezer for 40 to 45 minutes (see Step 3). The cheese filling can be used for stuffed shells, between lasagna layers, or dolloped in baked ziti.

1 pound ricotta cheese

1 pound mozzarella, cut fine or shredded

1 ¼ cups finely grated Parmesan cheese, plus more for baking and serving

4 large eggs, lightly beaten

½ cup finely chopped fresh parsley leaves

1 teaspoon coarse salt

¼ teaspoon freshly ground black pepper

2 to 3 dashes of Tabasco sauce

1 recipe Basic Italian Tomato Sauce (page 179)

1 recipe Man Crepes (page 38)

1 In a medium bowl, mix together the ricotta, mozzarella, Parmesan, eggs, parsley, salt, pepper, and Tabasco sauce.

2 Preheat the oven to 350°F. Spread some tomato sauce on the bottom of a 9 x 13 x 2-inch baking dish. One at a time, lay the crepes flat on a work surface and spread 3 tablespoons of the cheese mixture down the middle. Roll each crepe around the filling and place side by side in the pan. Spoon more tomato sauce over the crepes. Top with grated Parmesan.

3 Bake uncovered for 30 minutes, or until the sauce is bubbling and the crepes are heated through. Cool slightly and serve with additional warmed tomato sauce and grated Parmesan cheese on the side. ★

spicy indian chickpeas

serves 6 to 8

The alluring flavors of Indian food, laced with sweet spices, are an excellent introduction to more unusual ethnic tastes. This version of sweet-spiced chickpeas, with its robust, complex spice flavors, snares even the pickiest eaters. Hot or cold, this dish is an instant hit at every potluck it attends. Serve for lunch or dinner with either Indian-style bread such as naan or plain white rice, and accompany with the simple Cucumber Yogurt Salad on page 109.

2½ tablespoons vegetable oil

1 medium onion, finely chopped (about 1½ cups), plus 1 small onion, sliced, for garnish

8 garlic cloves, minced (2 tablespoons)

1 3-inch-square piece of peeled fresh ginger, minced (3 tablespoons)

1½ teaspoons ground cinnamon

1½ teaspoons garam masala

2 teaspoons ground cumin

1 teaspoon ground coriander

½ teaspoon ground cloves

¼ teaspoon cayenne pepper

2½ teaspoons coarse salt

2 tablespoons tomato paste

3 15-ounce cans chickpeas, drained (1 cup liquid reserved)

1 large tomato, sliced in wedges, for garnishing

3 hot fresh green chilies, sliced lengthwise and seeded, for garnishing

1 Heat a large skillet and swirl in the oil. Add the chopped onion, garlic, and ginger. Sauté until soft and lightly golden, 5 to 6 minutes.

2 In a small bowl, combine the cinnamon, garam masala, cumin, coriander, cloves, cayenne, and salt. Add to the onion mixture; cook and stir the spices to lightly toast, 1 to 2 minutes. Stir in the tomato paste and cook for another few minutes to combine. The color should be dark red.

3 Add the chickpeas plus the cup of reserved liquid. Stir to combine. Cover and cook over medium heat for 10 minutes, removing the cover in the last few minutes. Remove from the heat and let sit for a minute to allow the beans to soak up the spice flavors. Season with salt to taste.

4 Serve in a shallow bowl garnished with the sliced onion, tomato wedges, and slices of green chilies. *

cucumber yogurt salad
makes 3 cups

This cooling salad, known as raita, is served with many Indian dishes to temper spicy flavors. I like it with spicy chickpeas and rice or Indian bread as a complete meal. It's also great with chicken curry and mango chutney.

1 cucumber, peeled, seeded, and chopped (about 1 cup)

2 cups plain yogurt

1½ teaspoons toasted cumin seeds

½ teaspoon coarse salt

Pinch of cayenne pepper

Mix all ingredients together in a medium bowl. Chill and serve. *

PLAIN YOGURT

Keep a supply of plain yogurt in the refrigerator at the ready for smoothies, snacks, or quick salads. It aids in digestion by offering beneficial bacteria to our digestive systems and is an excellent source of calcium. Greek-style yogurt is thicker than other types, with a richer, more concentrated texture and flavor, which I prefer. If you're a big yogurt eater, try to buy organic, which doesn't contain BGH, the bovine growth hormone present in most conventional milk.

Some ideas for using yogurt:
- As the basis for smoothies or Indian lassi, a chilled yogurt drink made with water and crushed ice, and flavored with fruit or spices
- Mixed with maple syrup or jam for a quick snack
- Topped with berries and other fruits, a natural sweetener such as honey, and chopped nuts
- As a creamy base for salad dressings
- As an alternative to buttermilk for baking
- Drained for a spreadable alternative to cream cheese

CLOCKWISE FROM LEFT: Cucumber Yogurt Salad (this page) and Spicy Indian Chickpeas (page 107), served with jasmine rice

cheesy corn snack

makes 4 quarts

Many commercial versions of this snack are on the market, but this delicious homemade version which has all the attractive elements of the store-bought, and none of the toxins—just simple flavors made with fresh ingredients. My tallest brother consumed huge quantities of the homemade stuff while growing up, just to fill him up in between meals. Two hungry boys can easily devour this batch, but it will feed up to six normal people for a small snack. This recipe appeals to all ages. You can intensify it with ground pepper or other desired flavoring.

2 tablespoons vegetable oil

¾ cup popping corn kernels

4 tablespoons (½ stick) unsalted butter, melted

⅓ cup grated Parmesan cheese

½ teaspoon coarse salt

1 Heat a 4-quart pot with a tight-fitting lid on the stove top. Add the oil and swirl it around to coat the bottom of the pot. Get it hot enough to sizzle when a kernel hits the oil. Pour the corn in all at once, cover, and shake. Swirl the pot over the top of the burner once or twice until you hear the first few kernels pop. Once the corn is popping, swirl the pot continuously until the popping stops. Or, use a popcorn maker if you want to. Dump the popcorn into a large bowl.

2 Pour the melted butter over the corn and toss well to fully coat the kernels. Sprinkle the cheese and salt over the corn and toss until everything is well combined. ✳

basic salsa

makes 2 cups

This quick salsa can be used as a dip for tortilla chips or as a topping for eggs, tacos, chicken, or fish. It will keep in the refrigerator for a few days.

2 large tomatoes, cored and finely chopped

4 small radishes, halved and finely sliced

1 to 2 serrano or jalapeño peppers, sliced

⅓ cup finely chopped white onion

2 tablespoons chopped fresh cilantro

1 teaspoon coarse salt

½ cup water

Combine all ingredients in a medium bowl. Serve at room temperature or chilled. ✳

what's for dinner?

the most burning question

We all have this one meal in common.
While many skip breakfast, or are too busy for lunch,
everyone makes time for dinner. So make it happen
and show a little love, why don't you?

chicken answers

We eat a lot of chicken at home, and I know we aren't alone. Unless they've been raised vegetarian, your kids will eat a lot of chicken in their young lives, so buy and cook it well.

Chickens don't have fingers Processed chicken is pushed on kids from an early age in the form of "fingers," and because kids will ask for them, most parents capitulate, offering this ultraconvenient frozen food item—consisting of pressed-together chicken parts—as a regular weeknight meal. Stop! Your kids will get enough of these so-called fingers outside the home. Make a healthier homemade rendition using fresh chicken slices, dipped in egg and bread crumbs (page 117).

Have the butcher cut up whole birds or do it yourself. A whole chicken is cheaper and less processed, and it spreads itself much farther. Yes, I love wings and thighs and boneless breasts for certain things and buy them in packs if necessary. But the more a manufacturer has to do to an item before packaging, the more expensive it is.

Cutting apart a whole bird is a matter of finding that sweet spot in the joint through which to cut with a sharp knife. A good pair of kitchen shears makes quick work of cutting up both sides of the backbone and through the breastbone.

A bird can easily be cut into eight standard pieces. Sometimes, I cut each piece in half again to stretch a dish. For some preparations, simply removing the backbone and laying the chicken flat to cook (known as spatchcocking) is all that's needed for roasting or grilling. Save the backbones, neck bones, and wing tips in the freezer, and when you have enough, make chicken broth. Keep the cycle going of butchering whole chickens, reserving the bony parts, making stock, and resupplying both. I might immediately put the backbone and wing tips in water to boil for a light broth. In the time it takes to sauté the chicken, I have a flavorful liquid for deglazing.

You want to be careful when cutting and handling raw chicken, to avoid cross contamination. Lay down a piece of baking parchment or paper towel on the counter before working with it. Wash your counter, utensils, and hands with soap and hot water afterward.

cook and keep cooking

Learn to cook chicken with all its parts in many different styles: sautéing, braising, poaching, shallow-frying, roasting, grilling, and deep-frying.

● In the oven: A simple roast chicken cooks faster if you remove the backbone. This is a good choice if you're in a hurry: 40 minutes in a 400°F oven is better than one hour when folks are waiting to eat. See Flat Roast Chicken on page 120.

● On the grill: It's easier to manage a spatchcocked bird than many individual pieces. Prepare the grill. Salt and pepper the chicken. Place it skin side up. Cover and cook for 30 minutes. Turn the bird over, but to avoid breaking the skin, don't pivot it. Lift it gently with tongs and a spatula. Cover and cook for 20 more minutes. Generously brush with your favorite barbecue sauce. Turn and cook for 5 minutes. Sugary barbecue sauce will char your bird if left unmonitored. Watch the bird carefully in the last 10 minutes in order to nicely caramelize with the sauce, not burn it. Brush the opposite side with sauce. Cook for 5 more minutes. Remove from the grill. Let rest for 10 minutes. Cut into pieces and serve.

● In a pot: A 3- to 3½-pound bird, simmered in about 10 cups of water for 50 minutes, yields 2 quarts of chicken broth and 1 quart of shredded meat to use in salads, pot pies, soups, and sandwiches.

taste

There's nothing like the deep poultry taste of well-raised organic chicken, so seek birds that are the freshest and of the best quality possible, 3 to 4 pounds each, tops. Find out how the manufacturers harvest their birds; air-chilled rather than chilled in water is a cleaner process, which yields better-flavored birds. Sometimes I air-dry the skin before cooking (for a crisp skin) by patting the bird dry with a paper towel; if there's time, I refrigerate it without covering before seasoning. Cook the livers and kidneys for yourself or the dog.

As with all meats, remove the chicken from the refrigerator 30 minutes before cooking so that it cooks evenly and is less likely to dry out.

quick fried chicken

serves 4

Fried chicken on the table in forty-five minutes? Here it is, the quick recipe. I serve it with Chunky Mashed Potatoes (page 196) and Braised Collard Greens (page 212). The boys love it.

1 quart buttermilk or milk

2 tablespoons Tabasco or other hot sauce

1 3- to 3½-pound chicken, cut into 8 pieces and each breast cut in half again (reserve the neck, back, and wing tips for another purpose)

1 cup all-purpose flour

1½ teaspoons coarse salt, plus a little more for sprinkling

½ teaspoon freshly ground black pepper

¼ teaspoon cayenne pepper

2 cups peanut oil, vegetable oil, bacon fat, or lard

1 In a 9 x 13-inch baking dish, stir together the buttermilk and Tabasco. Submerge the chicken parts in the mixture and leave as long as possible, at least 10 minutes (but up to overnight—in the fridge—is even better).

2 In a plastic or paper bag, combine the flour, salt, black pepper, and cayenne.

3 Shake the chicken parts, 2 or 3 pieces at a time, in the flour. Repeat with the remaining chicken. Shake off the excess flour. In a 14-inch skillet (or two smaller skillets), heat 2 inches of oil over high heat until very hot. Test with a tiny bit of chicken skin. If the oil bubbles immediately, it is hot enough.

4 Place the chicken into the hot oil. Evenly distribute as many pieces as will fit in one layer in the pan, leaving ½ inch between pieces, and leave to fry undisturbed for about 15 minutes. Lower the heat as necessary to prevent excessive browning before the meat is cooked properly; the oil should continue to bubble steadily. Turn the pieces and cook for an additional 15 to 20 minutes.

5 Remove to a rack to drain. Repeat the process to cook all the chicken. To keep the first batch warm, place on a rimmed baking sheet in a 200°F oven. Sprinkle with salt and serve. *

miss lamie's fried chicken

serves 8

One of the best fried-chicken recipes I've encountered comes from Miss Lamie, of Westmoreland in Jamaica, who has happily cooked for more than her fair share of hungry men. The method used to fry the chicken certainly isn't conventional, and the seasoning creates fantastically deep flavor. Serve with her Tomato Onion Stew (page 210), boiled potatoes, and a fresh vegetable salad. It's also great for a picnic, eaten cold.

Two 3- to 4-pound chickens, cut into 8 pieces and each breast cut in half again (reserve the neck, back, and wing tips for another purpose)

3 teaspoons coarse salt

1½ teaspoons freshly ground black pepper

2 teaspoons dried thyme

2 onions, peeled and sliced

3 cups plain dried bread crumbs

2 large eggs, beaten

1½ to 2 cups vegetable oil

1 Place the chicken parts into a large bowl. Toss with 1½ teaspoons of the salt, pepper, thyme, and onions. Cover and let season in the fridge for at least 1 hour or up to overnight.

2 Spread the bread crumbs, combined with the remaining salt, out on a plate. Pour the eggs over the chicken, coating each piece completely. Roll each chicken piece in the bread crumbs. Discard the onions.

3 Heat a 14-inch skillet (or two smaller skillets) over high heat until a drop of water skitters around, then swirl 1 inch of oil into the pan. Reduce the heat to medium high, add the chicken pieces in a single layer, and fry until the chicken is well browned on all sides, about 30 to 40 minutes. Work in batches if necessary. Drain on paper towels and serve. ✳

PRESEASONING MEAT

Recipes such as this one rely on early seasoning to bring a big flavor punch into the meat. It's a good strategy for time management as well: If you have the meat on hand, season it in the morning or the night before and leave it to soak up all the flavor. No sauces or last-minute marinades and flavoring are needed for a delicious taste—just the final cooking. Meat can also be seasoned and then frozen when you first bring it home from the market. As the meat defrosts, the flavor will have even more time to intensify.

A Son's First Kitchen

While helping our oldest son get settled in his first apartment in Vermont, we took a break to go for a swim. On our way home from a remote swimming hole, we noticed a roadside farm. A hand-painted sign advertised: EAT LOCAL—FRESH CHICKEN, PORK, AND LAMB, so we stopped in to meet a gentleman farmer named Arthur. He raised the animals naturally on his farm, and sold the meat right there at his makeshift store. We chose small quantities of chicken, fresh pork, and bacon to stock our son's freezer, hoping that this would begin his departure from eating the unhealthy garbage offered at his college dining hall. Surely, he would prepare at least one healthful meal for himself using these local meats. As it turned out, he did so more than once—at least until the freezer was empty. And the meat purchase jump-started his interest in preparing his own home-cooked dinners, vegetables and all.

I put a few fresh tomatoes on his kitchen counter before I left. Of course, BLTs were his first meal. Next came roast chicken. ("Amazing," he proclaimed.) When he asked what to do with two cans of tuna, dry pasta, beets, and carrots, I suggested putting the beets and carrots on one baking sheet, tossing with olive oil, salt, pepper, and roasting in a 400°F oven. A quick tuna sauce (page 177) over pasta would work as well. Four college boys ate everything, everything, he said.

The next morning came a quick call on the way to class just to tell me of his breakfast. Corn, cut off the cob, sautéed in butter, chopped tomatoes, hardboiled eggs, and leftover greens.

The last call about the freezer items from Arthur's farm came several weeks later. "What's that thing you do with pork, apples, and onions?" he asked. Sauté and braise with a little cider or white wine, I tell him. He did it (see page 162). "Amazing," he said.

The last menu he told me about was reported after rather than before he cooked it. "Chicken piccata, basically from *The Joy of Cooking*," he said. "Salad made with veggies from Pete's grandmother's garden in upstate New York. Fusilli pasta with Costco pesto."

"What?" I said. "You didn't make your own pesto?"

"Mom," he said, "it was perfectly serviceable."

Every phone call, every question validated my instincts: Raise boys on fresh-cooked food, and they'll want to make it for themselves when they can. But, when they do, they'll make it their own way, not yours.

flat roast chicken

serves 4 to 6

How many times have I made roast chicken over the years? Thousands. How many ways? Too many to count, but every couple of years, I change my technique. Speed has become more and more of a concern—getting the food out fast to a horde of ravenous males. One day, in a rush, we simply cut the backbone out and laid the whole bird flat, seasoned it with salt and pepper, and cooked it in under an hour. Gone is the problem of the breast cooking before the rest; all the pieces cook evenly. If you wish, finish with a lemon sauce poured over after cooking, which tastes tangy and delicious over the crisp skin. An ovenproof 14-inch skillet, preferably cast-iron, makes for an easy job.

1 whole chicken, 3 to 4 pounds, backbone removed

Coarse salt and freshly ground black pepper

¼ cup extra-virgin olive oil

2 tablespoons unsalted butter

3 tablespoons fresh lemon juice

¼ teaspoon crushed red pepper flakes (optional)

2 garlic cloves, smashed and peeled (optional)

1 Preheat the oven to 400°F. Using kitchen shears, cut along both sides of the backbone to remove. Reserve it for broth. Open the chicken's legs and spread the bird down flat, skin side up. Press down firmly on the breastbone to flatten it. Pat it dry with paper towels. Salt and pepper generously on both sides.

2 Heat a large ovenproof skillet such as cast iron on high heat. Add 1 tablespoon of the olive oil and 1 tablespoon of the butter. Immediately add the chicken, skin side down. Allow to brown (without moving) for 3 minutes. Turn the chicken over, careful not to break the skin, and transfer the skillet to the oven.

3 The chicken is done when it is golden brown and cooked through, 40 to 45 minutes. An instant-read thermometer inserted in the thickest part, not touching bone, should read 165°F. Remove the chicken to a cutting board to rest for 10 minutes. Add 1 tablespoon of the lemon juice and the remaining tablespoon of butter to the pan drippings and swirl around.

4 Meanwhile, if you want to make the lemon sauce, whisk together the remaining 3 tablespoons of olive oil, 2 tablespoons of the lemon juice, the red pepper flakes, garlic, and a pinch of salt. Cut the chicken into pieces, drizzle with the pan sauce and the optional fresh lemon sauce, and serve immediately. *

Roasting pan method: Follow Step 1, then place the chicken in a large, shallow roasting pan, skin side up, and put in the oven. Proceed to Step 3 and complete.

baked chicken with
honey—whole-grain mustard glaze

serves 4

One Valentine's Day, I received a text message from my oldest son, Calder: <just made an amazing dinner>. Calder's menu (re-created here) reflects a little bit of what he's learned from both parents—from Mom, a balanced meal of meat, starch, and a fresh, subtly flavored salad; from Dad, big, rich, buttery deliciousness infused wherever possible. Noteworthy is the way it was written down, which is a clue to how someone really thinks about cooking food outside the convention of "normal" recipe writing. My favorite part is the instruction to "make sure you save all those delicious, lemony, chickeny juices that collected in the pan." Later on in his notes, he writes that he "took the juices that had collected and poured them on top of the potato mixture and fried the top with the scalding oil."

8 chicken thighs

½ cup olive oil (maybe more)

1 lemon (juiced)

Salt and pepper to taste

Some fresh herbs (if you have them)

FOR THE GLAZE

1 tablespoon whole-grain mustard (I also used maple mustard and a little Dijon)

1 or 2 tablespoons honey

⅓ cup olive oil

A little salt and pepper

1 Marinate chicken in olive oil, lemon juice, salt, pepper, and herbs, for at least 1 hour and up to a day in advance. Preheat oven to 375°F. Rub big baking pan with olive oil or butter, place thighs skin side down.

2 Bake for 20 to 25 minutes and turn skin side up. Bake for 10 more minutes. To make the glaze, add mustard, honey, and oil in a bowl in that order, whisk, add salt and pepper, whisk some more. Apply glaze with brush or spoon and broil for 5 minutes.

3 Take out and let rest for a second and make sure you save all those delicious, lemony, chickeny juices that collected in the pan. ⋆

Hash Browns

2 tablespoons olive oil

1 tablespoon butter

1 quarter onion, minced

1 whole potato, boiled and shredded

Salt and pepper

Heat pan on medium-high, add oil and butter. When the fat is heated add minced onion, cook until soft; add shredded potato and salt and pepper, stir, and mix up. Then start pressing the mixture down and toward the center of the pan. Try to get it to congeal and keep pressing it down and cook for 10 to 12 minutes while occasionally lifting the mixture so it doesn't stick. When I took the meat out I took the juices that had collected and poured them on top of the potato mixture and fried the top with the scalding oil—it was amazing. Cut into two or more pieces. *

Salad with Three-Mustard Vinaigrette

Boston lettuce

1 red onion

Sliced cucumber

(Whatever vegetables sound good, maybe not the cucumber)

DRESSING

½ tablespoon each of whole-grain, maple, and Dijon mustard

A little honey

Some lemon juice

A couple tablespoons olive oil

Salt and pepper

(Again, maybe a fresh herb minced as well)

Mix veggies, then add a little dressing to each individual portion *

chicken and dumplings

serves 6

What's better than cozy comfort food, straight from the American heartland? This one-pot meal yields a savory and satisfying dinner, and it's perfect for a large family of boys who need stick-to-the-ribs food. Halfway between soup and stew, crowned with light and fluffy herb-flecked dumplings, it's the best of both worlds. I love adding parsnips and turnips, but if you're root-vegetable averse you can leave them out and substitute cut-up raw potatoes. Many recipes from the American South even call for adding a sliced-up hard-boiled egg to the pot! Serve this with a green salad dressed with Green Goddess Ranch Salad Dressing (see page 98).

1 3- to 4-pound chicken

1 onion, halved but root end left intact

1 large carrot, coarsely chopped

1 celery stalk, coarsely chopped

4 sprigs of fresh parsley

1 turnip, trimmed and chopped

2 parsnips, coarsely chopped

8 to 10 cups water

1 tablespoon coarse salt

DUMPLINGS

1 cup all-purpose flour

2 teaspoons baking powder

½ teaspoon coarse salt

¾ cup milk

1 teaspoon chopped fresh dill or parsley

1. To make the chicken, place the chicken into a large pot with a tight-fitting lid. Add the onion, carrot, celery, parsley, turnip, and parsnips to the pot and barely cover with the water.

2. Bring to a boil over high heat, reduce the heat to a simmer, partially cover, and simmer for 50 minutes. Lift out the chicken and vegetables. Discard the onion halves and parsley sprigs. Continue to simmer the broth for 15 to 20 minutes. Add the salt. When the chicken is cool enough to handle, remove the meat from the bones and shred into large pieces. You'll have 4 cups of shredded chicken. Use 2 to 4 cups as desired.

3. To make the dumplings, in a small bowl, whisk together the flour, baking powder, and salt. Stir in the milk and dill or parsley to combine.

4. Drop the dough, 1 tablespoon at a time, onto the simmering broth. Cover and cook until the dumplings have cooked through, 3 to 4 minutes. Carefully return the shredded chicken and the vegetables to the pot. Reheat for 1 minute. Serve in wide bowls with big spoons. *

American Dumplings There are a couple of different camps when it comes to the "right" type of dumpling for chicken and dumplings. This recipe calls for the light, fluffy dropped dumplings, made in a few minutes, which float on top. Other versions use the firmer rolled dumplings, which look like noodles ribboned throughout the pot; they're made from egg, flour, water, and salt and are formed into a dough that usually requires a couple hours' or an overnight rest before rolling out and boiling.

crunchy sesame chicken wings

makes 20 wings

I will fight for the wings every time a whole chicken is served for dinner. Unfortunately, I raised boys who also want them, so now and then we need to have all-wing dinners. For us wing-lovers, wings—as a main dish or snacking food—are pure heaven. I especially like when the wing tip is extra crispy and I can chew it down to the end, like a potato chip. My husband started cutting them off and cooking them separately to snack on, which also allows more wings to fit on a baking sheet. Wings can also be separated in 2 for smaller portions, detatching the drumette at the joint. Serve with a bottle of hot sauce at the table.

20 chicken wings

3 large eggs, beaten

Vegetable oil, for coating the pan

½ cup sesame seeds

½ cup all-purpose flour

2 teaspoons coarse salt

¼ teaspoon cayenne pepper

½ cup fresh bread crumbs

2 to 3 garlic cloves, minced

Hot sauce, for serving

1 Preheat the oven to 375°F. Place the chicken wings in a large bowl. Add the eggs and toss to coat. Line a large rimmed baking sheet with baking parchment or coat the pan with oil.

2 In a small bowl, combine the sesame seeds, flour, salt, cayenne, bread crumbs, and garlic. Dip each wing into the sesame mixture to fully coat. Place the coated wings side by side on the prepared baking sheet.

3 Bake for 30 minutes and increase the temperature to 400°F. Cook until the wings are golden brown and sizzling, 20 to 30 more minutes. Immediately remove the wings from the baking sheet while hot. Serve with hot sauce. ⋆

vinegar glossed chicken

serves 6 to 8

This dish has been in heavy rotation in our home as a favorite weeknight dinner option for at least twenty years. Originally made from an Italian recipe of unknown origin, it has morphed into our own, though my husband and I each make it a little differently. This much is certain, however: when the rosemary vinegar is added to the pan of golden browned chicken, alchemy occurs as the vinegar deglazes those brown bits and reduces itself into a syrup. It permeates each chicken piece with an *agrodolce* (sweet-and-sour) flavor. There's no better accompaniment than polenta, soft and loose or firm and sliced. It's a heavenly combination of textures and flavors. (Rice, pasta, or bread will also work, as long as there is something to sop up the sauce.) Like many of the dishes here, it only improves when made in advance.

1 cup best-quality red wine vinegar

2 to 3 garlic cloves, minced
(about 2 tablespoons)

3 sprigs of fresh rosemary, chopped
(about 1 tablespoon)

5½ pounds bone-in chicken pieces
(each part should be cut in half)

Coarse salt and freshly ground black pepper

Extra-virgin olive oil

¾ cup chicken broth, plus more as needed

1 At least 15 minutes but up to 2 hours before cooking, combine the vinegar, garlic, and rosemary to marinate.

2 Thoroughly season the chicken pieces with salt and pepper. Heat a 14-inch skillet (or two smaller skillets) over high heat and swirl in enough olive oil to coat the bottom of the skillet. Place the chicken in the skillet, skin side down. Don't crowd the chicken; leave space around each piece. Work in batches if necessary. You should hear an immediate sizzle when the chicken pieces hit the pan. Don't move them; it takes a couple minutes to sear the chicken so it doesn't stick. Brown all sides; this will take 10 minutes per batch. Regulate the heat so it stays high but does not burn the chicken. Place all the browned chicken back in the skillet.

3 Add the chicken broth and scrape up any brown bits from the bottom of the pan. Lower the heat, simmer, and reduce for 15 to 20 minutes. Increase the heat to high and pour in the vinegar mixture. Swirl the pan and stir around as the vinegar evaporates to form a simmering glaze, 8 to 10 minutes. Serve immediately or reheat with some extra broth. ★

Polenta

A staple of northern Italian cooking, polenta is boiled cornmeal. It's traditionally slow-cooked and requires constant stirring. But the modern-style instant polenta that's readily available at grocery stores works better for time-pressed home cooking. Once cooked, polenta firms up as it cools, so it can be shaped or molded and then sliced and reheated at mealtime. Pour the loose hot polenta into a greased loaf pan, smooth the top with a spoon, cover, and chill. When ready to serve, slice the polenta, panfry the slices in olive oil, or warm them in the oven or microwave. The hot polenta also can be poured into a greased rimmed baking sheet, spread evenly, covered, and chilled. When it is set, it can be cut into shapes with round, square, or diamond shaped biscuit cutters. Many stores also carry a premade log of polenta, in the dairy case, ready to be sliced and heated.

stir-fried chinese chicken and peanuts

serves 2 to 4

This home-style version of kung pao chicken and peanuts holds a special place in my recipe file as the first quasi-authentic Chinese dish I mastered. Serve with lots of steamed white rice. Other accompaniments for a full menu are Cold Sesame Noodles (page 104) and Chinese Celery Salad (page 103). For more servings, stir-fry an additional batch; don't double up in one pan unless you have a huge wok!

⅓ cup soy sauce

3 tablespoons shaoxing cooking wine or dry sherry

1 tablespoon rice vinegar or white vinegar

½ teaspoon sugar

½ teaspoon toasted sesame oil

1 whole boneless, skinless chicken breast (about 1½ pounds)

1½ tablespoons peanut oil or vegetable oil

¾ cup unsalted dry-roasted peanuts or cashews

2 whole scallions, thinly sliced

4 whole dried Chinese red peppers

2 garlic cloves, minced

1 tablespoon cornstarch

1 In a bowl, whisk together the soy, wine, vinegar, sugar, and sesame oil. Dice the chicken and toss it in the marinade.

2 Heat a wok or skillet over high heat until very hot. Add the oil. Lightly fry the peanuts for about 1 minute and remove. Add the scallions, red peppers, and garlic. Stir-fry for about 20 seconds.

3 Just before adding to the pan, coat the chicken in the cornstarch. Fry until the chicken is just cooked through, 3 to 4 minutes (depending on the pan and the heat). Return the peanuts to the pan and mix thoroughly to combine with the chicken. Serve immediately with white rice. ✳

Stir-Frying Stir-frying requires only a good wok or sauté pan, a long-handled spatula, some protein or vegetables, a heat source, and oil. Whenever making a stir-fry, set the table, including the drinks, and prepare all the ingredients in advance; then start to stir-fry at the last minute. Use the highest heat possible and work fast in order to cook the food without "steaming" it and losing moisture. Work in batches; don't overcrowd the pan.

note Food allergies, especially to peanut products, are a serious issue when feeding kids. Most parents identify them early on and take precautions to educate their families. Be mindful of young guests at your table who may require protection from a food allergy.

chicken parmesan

serves at least 6

You can prepare the sauce and chicken in the morning, then assemble the dish and pop it in the oven just before dinner. With spaghetti, sautéed spinach, and warm crusty bread, it makes a perfect Sunday dinner.

¼ cup extra-virgin olive oil

2 garlic cloves, minced

Pinch of crushed red pepper flakes

1 28-ounce can tomatoes, lightly pulsed in a blender or food processor

2 teaspoons coarse salt

3 pounds boneless, skinless chicken breasts (3 whole breasts, split down the middle)

½ cup plain bread crumbs

¾ cup freshly grated Parmesan cheese

¼ teaspoon freshly ground black pepper

1 tablespoon unsalted butter, plus more if needed

1½ pounds fresh mozzarella cheese, sliced thin

1. Heat a saucepan over medium-high heat and add 1 tablespoon of the olive oil, the garlic, and the red pepper flakes. Stir for 30 seconds. Add the tomatoes and ½ teaspoon of the salt. Simmer for 30 minutes.

2. Meanwhile, working on a large surface covered in baking parchment or plastic wrap, lay down the chicken breasts. Using a sharp slicing knife, cut each piece in half horizontally through the middle.

3. In a large prep pan or dish, combine the bread crumbs and ½ cup of the Parmesan cheese. Spread out to cover the whole bottom of the pan. Lay down as many chicken breasts as will fit on the mixture. Sprinkle salt and pepper over each piece and turn over, completely coating with the bread-crumb mixture. Repeat the process with the remaining pieces of chicken.

4. Heat a large skillet over medium-high heat. Swirl in 2 tablespoons of olive oil, along with the butter, to coat the pan. Add the chicken breasts in one layer and cook until golden, about 3 minutes on each side. Remove and repeat the process for the remaining chicken, adding a little oil and butter to the pan as needed.

5. Preheat the oven to 400°F. Spoon some tomato sauce into a greased 9 x 13-inch baking dish to cover. Layer in the chicken pieces and top with mozzarella slices. Spoon over about 1¼ cups more sauce, and sprinkle on the remaining ¼ cup of Parmesan cheese. Bake until golden and bubbling, 30 to 35 minutes. Let rest for at least 15 minutes before serving. ★

Sunday-Night Supper

Do you dread Sunday evenings as the last of the weekend gives way to thoughts of Monday-morning work or school routine? Stretch the day by making a crowd-pleasing dinner that leaves you time to enjoy it. Choose a dish like this one, which can be prepared the morning of and finished before dinner, or a long-simmering roast such as Asian-Style Pork Roast (page 161) or Luscious Oven-Braised Short Ribs (page 143), which cook slowly throughout the day, letting their intoxicating scent waft through the house as a pleasant promise of the coming meal.

chicken enchiladas salsa verde

serves 6

I know this enchilada casserole is a winner, because my dad, who (unlike most other men) "hated" Mexican food, fell in love with it. If you're pressed for time, use a store-bought green sauce (made from tomatillos) and shredded store-bought rotisserie chicken for a quicker version of this dish. These bubbling, subtle-tasting enchiladas are even better with a cool, crunchy salad on top.

GREEN SAUCE

½ white onion, peeled and coarsely chopped

2 garlic cloves, unpeeled

2 serrano or jalapeño chilies, stems removed

14 whole tomatillos, peeled and simmered in water for 5 minutes

¼ cup unsalted roasted peanuts

2 teaspoons coarse salt

½ cup chicken broth

ENCHILADAS

1 tablespoon vegetable oil, plus 2 teaspoons more for dressing the salad

3 cups green sauce

12 corn tortillas, toasted, stacked, and wrapped in a clean kitchen towel to steam (see page 22)

4 cups shredded chicken (from a 3-pound poached chicken; see Savory Chicken Pocket Pies, page 62, for poaching instructions)

7 ounces queso fresco, crumbled, or shredded Monterey Jack cheese

3 to 4 cups shredded romaine lettuce, washed and dried

6 radishes, trimmed and sliced

1 teaspoon white vinegar

Coarse salt and freshly ground black pepper

1 To make the sauce, preheat the broiler. Place the onion, garlic, and chilies on a baking sheet. Broil for 4 minutes, or until charred and blistered. Discard the garlic skin. Place the onion, garlic, and chilies in a blender jar with the tomatillos, peanuts, salt, and broth. Blend until smooth.

2 Preheat the oven to 375°F.

3 To make the enchiladas, heat a saucepan to medium high and add the tablespoon of oil. Carefully pour in the green sauce and cook, stirring constantly to thicken up, about 3 minutes. One by one dip the tortillas in the sauce, place in an ungreased 9 x 13-inch baking dish, fill with some chicken, and roll up. Fit each enchilada snugly next to the other in the baking dish. Pour the remaining green sauce over the enchiladas. Sprinkle the cheese on top. Bake for 15 minutes, or until the sauce is bubbling and the enchiladas are heated through.

4 Meanwhile, toss the lettuce and radishes with the remaining 2 teaspoons of oil, the vinegar, and salt and pepper. Layer the salad on top of the hot enchiladas and serve immediately. ∗

mexican wrappers, noodles, or chips

Many Mexican dishes use corn or flour tortillas in different guises (see page 22).

- **Corn tortillas** are thin, round pancakes of unleavened corn dough. Dry corn kernels are cooked, soaked, and ground to a smooth dough called masa, then formed into a ball, pressed, and cooked on a hot ungreased griddle until lightly speckled brown but still soft and pliable.

- **Flour tortillas** are staples of Northern Mexico, Texas, and Southwest cooking, and are made of flour, lard (or other fat), salt, and water. For thicker Tex-Mex style tortillas, baking powder is added. Dough is rolled into small balls, rested, and pressed on a tortilla press or rolled out with a rolling pin and cooked on a skillet or griddle.

- **Burritos** are wheat-flour tortillas filled with a combination of beans and/or meat, cheese, and salsa, then folded and wrapped to resemble a *burro* ("little donkey").

- **Enchiladas** are made with corn tortillas—sometimes dipped in sauce first, sometimes not—that are rolled around a filling, topped with sauce and cheese, and usually baked. Another traditional method involves a quick dip in hot fat, then sauce, before being filled and rolled, but this is best if the enchiladas are eaten as soon as they are made.

- **Tacos** are hot toasted corn tortillas wrapped around shredded meat or beans and doused with salsa, such as the Basic Salsa on page 110. Less desirable, yet kid-friendly, preformed hard taco shells can be filled with desired fillings

TOMATILLOS

Small Mexican green ground-cherry tomatillos are covered in a papery husk that is removed before use. They have a slightly acidic lemony flavor and can be used raw, boiled, or roasted in sauces and salads. Most commercially available green salsas are made from tomatillos, which can also substitute for freshly made green salsa if called for in a recipe. Look for fresh ones in the produce section of your market or for canned ones in the international foods section.

brined and oven-roasted turkey

serves 10 to 12 generously

No matter how many times you tackle a holiday bird, it can seem like your first. You root around for a recipe or try to remember a familiar technique. I've cooked turkey many ways over the years. My favorite is barbecued on a Weber kettle grill—see page 138. My second choice is brining the bird before roasting it in the oven. This method is especially good if you're a novice cook, allowing for some leeway by adding moisture to the bird and making it harder to overcook and dry out.

Don't forget that turkey makes a welcome addition to a buffet table in any season. If you have to feed a large crowd, it's a fantastic choice. Always pick the best-quality bird available to you.

BRINING LIQUID

2 quarts (8 cups) water (at the very least)

1½ cups coarse salt

½ cup sugar

1 large red onion, sliced

1 head of garlic, smashed (8 to 10 cloves)

2 bottles white wine

BRINE ADD-INS (OPTIONAL)

2 tablespoons crushed black peppercorns

2 teaspoons crushed red pepper flakes

2 teaspoons dried coriander

1 tablespoon dried fennel

1 tablespoon dried cumin

1 whole cinnamon stick

5 whole cloves

4 bay leaves

4 large sprigs of fresh sage

TURKEY

1 16-pound turkey (approximate)

1 recipe Sausage Bread Stuffing (page 140)

Extra-virgin olive oil

Coarse salt and freshly ground black pepper

TURKEY GRAVY

⅓ cup all-purpose flour

3 to 4 cups turkey or chicken broth

Pan drippings from 1 roasted turkey, reserved in the roasting pan

SPECIAL EQUIPMENT

5-gallon bucket (for brining)

Trussing supplies or needle and string

Roasting pan

1. In a 2-quart pot, bring 1 quart of water to a boil with the salt and sugar, stirring occasionally until the salt and sugar have dissolved. Cool completely and place in a clean 5-gallon bucket with the onion, garlic, wine, and any of the optional spices or herbs. Stir in the remaining water completely to combine. Add the turkey. Cover and store in a cold place for at least 12 hours and up to 24 hours. Turn bird occasionally

2. Drain the turkey, pat dry, and bring to room temperature an hour before cooking. Preheat the oven to 375°F.

3. Stuff the cavity and neck of the bird with the stuffing. Truss or tie the cavity closed. Tuck the wings under the breast and place in the roasting pan. Rub the bird all over with olive oil, salt, and pepper. Roast the bird for 2 to 3 hours, or until an instant-read thermometer in the thickest part of a leg reaches 165°F. After 1 hour, baste every 30 minutes with pan juices. After 2 hours, lower the oven temperature to 350°F. Let the turkey rest for at least 20 minutes before carving.

4. In a jar with a lid, shake the flour together with 1 cup of the broth. Place the pan with drippings over medium heat until it begins to bubble. Whisk in the flour mixture. Cook to thicken, 1 to 2 minutes. Add the remaining broth and simmer to reach desired thickness. Strain through a cheesecloth-lined sieve. Serve with the roasted turkey. ∗

NOTE: Trussing a turkey closes the cavity by either sewing the skin over the stuffing or sealing it altogether with skewers.

weber barbecued turkey

serves a crowd

If you have access to a charcoal grill, this recipe will yield the most amazing turkey over and over again. It's "Webered" outside, a boon for those of us at Thanksgiving who need a turkey-free oven for baking the majority of the dishes. But, these specialties could be all a guy needs for a lifetime of praise! This is a tried-and-true formula, perfected by our friend Lee, who has a pretty lean cooking repertoire: he's got it right down to the amount of coals called for, so don't deviate.

1 18- to 22-pound turkey, rinsed and patted dry (1 hour at room temperature)

1 recipe Sausage Bread Stuffing (page 140)

½ cup extra-virgin olive oil

½ cup coarse salt

2½ tablespoons freshly ground black pepper

SPECIAL EQUIPMENT

Trussing supplies or needle and string

1 chimney starter for coals

1 bag best-quality charcoal

1 disposable heat-proof aluminum roasting pan

1 stand-up Weber kettle grill with lid

1 Stuff the turkey with the sausage bread stuffing or your favorite stuffing and tie the cavity closed. In a chimney starter, ignite 50 charcoal briquettes and burn until they are ash gray. Center the roasting pan on the small bottom grate of the Weber. Divide the coals evenly on both outer sides of the roasting pan. (Be careful not to spill ashes into the pan since it will collect the turkey drippings.) Top with the grill grate.

2 In a small bowl, combine the olive oil, salt, and pepper. Rub all over the turkey. Place the bird on top of the grill, directly over the roasting pan, and cover. Add 8 charcoal briquettes on either side of the roasting pan every 45 minutes to keep the heat even. (Some grills have a grill grate with openings on the sides. Otherwise you'll need a helper to lift the grate with bird while you add the coals.) The bird is cooked in 3 to 4 hours depending on its size. An instant-read thermometer, inserted in a thigh joint, should read 165°F. Remove from the heat and let rest for at least 20 minutes before carving. ∗

Grilling

Grilling is a man's world, so if you're cooking for or with boys, some kind of an outdoor grill setup is a must. Learn to grill with them or for them—but learn to grill. It's an essential skill for boys on their way to becoming men who cook.

There are two basic kinds of heat sources and devices for grilling, with a gas or a charcoal grill. I like charcoal since food cooked on it undeniably produces a more authentic barbecue flavor. The setup and cleanup require more time and attention along with a greater mess. Charcoal briquettes or hardwood lump charcoal must first be ignited in the grill and left to burn until ash gray—about 15 minutes—before the grill is ready to use.

A gas grill gets fueled by a propane gas tank, which attaches to the grill and must be replenished from your local store as needed. Ignited with an automatic switch, a gas grill needs to be turned on just a few minutes before cooking, and aside from the cooking grate, cleanup is a snap. Gas grilling is a more convenient and efficient experience for the griller although much less fun (to some) without the dirt and smell of burning charcoal wafting through the air.

The Setup
The cooking methods are
- Direct heat: Food is cooked directly over the fire. Think burger or steak.
- Indirect heat: The hot coals or gas fire are confined to one side of the grill while the food is cooked "indirectly" on the side without the fire underneath, such as for turkey, chicken (not always), ribs, and brisket.

The Equipment
- Rather than having just one big grill, consider trying a couple of smaller ones, too, perhaps of different shapes. A kettle and a hibachi can serve different styles and sizes of grilling projects, and they're easily transportable to park or beach and not too hard to store if your space is limited. Smoke ribs slowly over indirect heat on a kettle style, or grill steaks directly over the hot flame of a hibachi.
- A good-fitting cover is important for temperature control and success.
- A chimney starter easily ignites the charcoal without the need for (lighter fluid–coated) instant "matchlight" charcoal, which invariably imparts a nasty smell and taste to the food.
- A grate cleaner, tongs, and a heavy-duty oven mitt are indispensable.
- A water source really completes your setup.

Never start a fire or light a grill without identifying the closest and most accessible water source—something I learned after a close call.

The Cleanup
- After the grill fully cools, take a minute to empty the ashes and debris. No one wants to begin a grilling project with someone else's mess.
- Scrape down the grates. Cover and store the grill, and restock any items that are running low. Nothing is worse than finding your supply of charcoal or gas empty as you're about to grill.

Tips for Success
- Most important, get the coals or heating element as hot as possible. Control the heat down from there by manipulating with vents and covering as needed. Too little heat from a fire, unless at the tail end of a roaring one, is a sorry affair.
- Sauces are usually applied toward the end of cooking so the meat has a chance to cook on its own without fire flare-ups from the sauce's ingredients.
- When barbecuing poultry, it's better to overcook than to undercook.
- Use an instant-read thermometer, a ten-dollar tool that reads the doneness of meat.

sausage bread stuffing

stuffs a 16- to 20-pound turkey

If you prefer bread stuffing, just omit the sausage.

1 tablespoon extra-virgin olive oil

1 pound sweet Italian sausage, casing removed

2 tablespoons unsalted butter

1 onion, chopped

3 celery stalks, sliced on the bias

2 garlic cloves, minced

1 heaping tablespoon minced fresh sage leaves, or 1 teaspoon crumbled dried sage

1 cup white wine

1 whole loaf bread, crusts removed, cubed (5 to 6 cups)

1 cup chicken broth

½ to 1 teaspoon coarse salt (depends on saltiness of sausage)

1 Heat a large skillet, add the olive oil, and cook the sausage, stirring and breaking it up until browned, about 8 minutes. Remove to a plate.

2 Add the butter to the skillet and when it melts, add the onion and celery. Sauté until the onion is translucent, 3 to 5 minutes. Stir in the garlic and sage and cook for 1 minute. Pour in the wine and deglaze the pan, stirring up any browned bits with a wooden spoon.

3 Add the cubed bread to the mixture and toast and turn a bit. Stir in the cooked sausage, the chicken broth, and salt to taste and cook for 1 minute. Cool the mixture. (This can be done quickly by spreading the mixture on a rimmed cookie sheet and chilling it in the refrigerator.)

4 Stuff the mixture into the cavity and neck of a cooked turkey, or place it in a large buttered baking dish and bake at 375°F for 25 minutes, or until browned on top and heated through. ∗

spiced cranberry sauce

makes 3 cups

Every turkey dinner (and leftover turkey sandwich) needs some form of cranberry sauce—even if it's just the classic one on the back of the fresh cranberry package. But this spicy version is also a great accompaniment for any plain roast chicken or pork dish.

1 cup water

1 medium orange, washed and dried

1 lemon, washed and dried

3 cups fresh cranberries (1 12-ounce package)

2 cups sugar

¾ teaspoon ground cinnamon

½ teaspoon ground cloves

1 Place ½ cup of the water in a blender jar. Cut the orange and lemon into eighths, keeping the peel but removing all seeds.

2 Blend half the orange and lemon pieces for 10 seconds. Add half the cranberries and blend just until the mixture is a coarse chop. Place in a saucepan. Repeat with the remaining water, orange and lemon wedges, and cranberries, and add the mixture to the pan.

3 Add the sugar, cinnamon, and cloves to the pan. Bring to a boil over high heat, reduce the heat, and simmer for 10 minutes, or until the sugar is dissolved and the flavors blended. Cool to room temperature and serve. The sauce will keep, covered, in the refrigerator for 2 weeks. ∗

luscious oven-braised short ribs

serves 6

Most recipes for short ribs tell you to brown the meat on the stove top before adding the braising liquid and cooking it. This recipe doesn't, eliminating the mess, time, and attention that this step requires. The ribs do their own work in the oven while you putter around doing something else. Add the potatoes in the last forty-five minutes, or omit them and serve the ribs with noodles, rice, or polenta if you prefer. The meat in its sauce turns out luscious.

1 onion, finely sliced

4 garlic cloves, smashed

1 leek, cleaned and finely chopped

1 carrot, finely chopped

1 celery stalk, finely chopped

4 sprigs of fresh thyme, or 1 teaspoon dried thyme

1 cup red wine

½ cup soy sauce or tamari

1 tablespoon sugar

¼ teaspoon freshly ground black pepper

3½ pounds short ribs

2 to 3 Idaho potatoes, peeled and cut in quarters (optional)

1 Mix all ingredients except the meat and potatoes in a 9 x 15-inch roasting pan. Add the ribs and rub all over with the marinade. The meat should fit comfortably in a single layer in the pan. Cover and let marinate in the refrigerator for 6 hours or up to overnight. Occasionally turn the meat over in the marinade. Remove from the refrigerator 30 minutes prior to cooking.

2 Preheat the oven to 400°F. Braise the short ribs for 2½ to 3 hours, reducing the heat to 350°F after an hour. Turn the ribs over. Add the potatoes in the last 40 minutes of cooking. Add water to the pan if too much liquid evaporates. You want to end up with glistening ribs in a reduced glaze. ✶

Short Ribs

Cooked properly, these wide, rectangular bone-in ribs (separated) are covered in flavor-producing soft tissue and fat that melts away during braising to infuse the sauce. They're almost guaranteed to become a guy's fondest food dream. Buy them in the meat section or place an order with the butcher.

grilled hanger steak

serves 6

You can't beat a flavorful marinade for steak, especially for a cut like hanger, which has a wonderful toothsome texture. Its compact narrow, half-foot-long pieces make it easy to maneuver around a small grill. To serve, slice it on the bias, against the grain. With potatoes and vegetables, a little goes a long way in serving the boys.

¾ cup red wine

2 tablespoons Worcestershire sauce

1 tablespoon Dijon mustard

1 tablespoon sugar

½ teaspoon freshly ground black pepper, plus more for grilling

2 pounds hanger steak, London broil, or sirloin

5 garlic cloves, smashed and peeled

Coarse salt

1 In a dish large enough to hold the meat, whisk together the wine, Worcestershire sauce, mustard, sugar, and pepper. Rub the meat with the garlic and place both in the marinade. Turn the meat to coat completely with the marinade. Cover and chill for at least 2 hours and up to overnight.

2 Bring the meat to room temperature. Prepare an outdoor grill or heavy sauté pan. Remove the meat from the marinade and pat dry. Generously salt and pepper both sides. Place on the hot grill, cover, and cook for 4 minutes. Turn and cook for an additional 6 to 8 minutes for medium rare, 140°F on an instant-read thermometer. Let the meat sit for at least 5 minutes before carving. This can also be cooked under the broiler. ∗

Stretching Steak

It's much more economical to serve boys slices of a large marinated steak like London broil or sirloin rather than smaller individual cuts (save those for just the two of you). Beef up the side dishes: potatoes, such as Italian Fries (page 194), and a couple of vegetables, such as Creamed Spinach (page 213) and Grilled Portobello Mushroom Steaks (page 199).

Steak with Creamed Spinach (page 213) and Italian Fries (page 194)

pan-fried steak

serves 2

If you want to cook at home for a guy you like, learn to make a pan-fried steak. That and crusty bread slathered in softened butter plus a bottle of red wine or cold beer are all you need to make him happy. Serve potatoes, such as Hash Browns (page 123), and a simple vegetable, such as steamed broccoli (see page 193), and he'll know you really care. Serve pie for dessert (see pages 223–229), and he'll be yours forever.

2 strip steaks (about 1 inch thick)

Coarse salt and freshly ground black pepper

1 to 2 teaspoons unsalted butter

1 Bring the steaks to room temperature.

2 Heat a 10- or 12-inch cast-iron skillet over high heat. Season the steaks liberally with salt and pepper. Seconds before adding a steak, drop ½ teaspoon of the butter into the pan and immediately top with the steak. Repeat with the remaining steak. Sear for 3 minutes without moving the steak (in order to form a crust). Turn and cook for 2 minutes for rare or for 3 to 4 for medium rare. Remove the steaks from the pan and let them rest on a board or platter for a few minutes before serving. *

SIMPLE STEAK SAUCE

Men love A1 Steak Sauce, HP Sauce, or bottled hot sauce, mustard, or horseradish with steak. So don't worry if you're afraid to make sauce; you can buy it. But, if you want to make a simple pan sauce, it's easy. Once the steak is removed from the pan, keep the heat on high and pour about ⅓ cup liquid (red or white wine, vinegar, vermouth, cognac, Armagnac, scotch, whiskey) into the hot pan, then scrape up the golden crusty bits that have formed on the bottom of the pan and let the mixture simmer for a few minutes to reduce. If using a gas flame, be careful of a flame-up, which should burn off quickly. Swirl in a couple tablespoons of thickener (butter, cream, creamy cheese, or mustard) and simmer for a minute more. Plate your steak (on a warmed plate) and pour over the sauce. The choice of liquid and thickener is a matter of taste.

We like these combinations: ● Wine and mustard ● Cognac and cream ● Armagnac and blue cheese ● Scotch whiskey and butter

steak pizzaiola

serves 6 to 8

For beef lovers, this dish delivers big-time flavor satisfaction. The caramelized tomatoey-beefy aroma when it is cooking is indescribably inviting and memorable. All you need are just a few ingredients and some time. The whole thing is cooked in one large ovenproof skillet, which works its magic untended once it is placed in the oven. When it's done the meat is easy to shred, with a robe of thickened tomato sauce clinging to it. Serve with bread or polenta and sautéed Swiss chard on the side. Or, present it as a "sauce," with all the meat shredded uniformly and tossed with a pound of big, boy-size pasta such as rigatoni and with a fluffy cloud of grated Parmesan cheese on top. This dish will never disappoint, and it could become your favorite dinner, both to make and to eat.

2½ pounds bone-in chuck steak, or 2 pounds if boneless

1 teaspoon coarse salt

Freshly ground black pepper

2 tablespoons extra-virgin olive oil

3 to 4 garlic cloves, minced

1 teaspoon dried oregano

1 teaspoon dried thyme

¼ teaspoon crushed red pepper flakes

1 tablespoon tomato paste

1 28-ounce can whole tomatoes, with juice

1. Preheat the oven to 325°F. Season the meat on both sides with salt and pepper. Heat a large ovenproof skillet over high heat and swirl in the olive oil. Brown the meat on both sides. Remove the meat from the skillet and take the pan off the heat.

2. Stir into the pan the garlic, oregano, thyme, red pepper flakes, tomato paste, and whole tomatoes. Mash up the tomatoes with the back of a spoon, return the meat to the pan, spoon the sauce over it, and cover tightly.

3. Braise in the oven for at least 2 hours, stirring occasionally. Uncover and cook for an additional 30 minutes, until the sauce has thickened up. *

Chuck Steak The secret of this dish is to use fatty meat with big bones, such as chuck steak, one of the most affordable and flavorful cuts of meat you can buy, which makes it perfect for guys. It's browned first, then slowly simmered in liquid until it becomes meltingly tender.

All Canned Tomatoes Are Not Created Equal Among available commercial brands, taste, acidity, and sweetness can vary. Muir Glen organic variety, my favorite, delivers a consistent, balanced flavor. Some of the imported Italian San Marzano tomatoes are excellent, too, but many others aren't. American brands are also of widely varied quality. Always taste your tomatoes first; if they have a strong acidic tang, then add up to ½ teaspoon of sugar per can to the tomatoes during cooking.

chili

serves 6

Different chili recipes present a wide variety of regional personalities and variations, not to mention favorites: Do you like it with or without beans? Chopped meat or ground meat? Whole chilies or mixed chili powder, or both? This recipe will appeal to just about everyone. Whether it's the Super Bowl, game night, or just a plain Tuesday dinner, it can be dressed up and down for the occasion. Always serve it with some combination of fixings, such as grated cheese, sour cream, sliced avocados, chopped tomatoes, chopped onion or scallions, or minced cilantro. Garnish with salty tortilla chips or crumble in corn bread.

5 dried red chilies (Mexican ancho, New Mexican Hatch, or Anaheim)

1 tablespoon olive oil

1 cup chopped onion

3 garlic cloves, minced (1 tablespoon)

2 pounds ground beef

1 tablespoon coarse salt

1 teaspoon ground cumin

¼ teaspoon crushed red pepper flakes, or pinch of cayenne pepper

½ teaspoon dried oregano

1 bay leaf

¼ cup pickled jalapeños, chopped (optional)

1 28-ounce can tomatoes, broken up, with juice

12 ounces beer

1 15-ounce can beans (pinto, kidney, black, or a combination), drained

Dried Red Chilies

If you dry a fresh green poblano chili, you wind up with a red Mexican ancho chili. Its flavor—earthy and mildly spicy yet slightly fruity—lends a marvelous depth to chili, sauces, and stews. New Mexican Hatch or dried red Anaheim chilies can also be used in place of ancho.

1 In a dry large skillet over high heat, lightly toast both sides of the chilies for a few minutes. After roasting, remove from pan to slice open, then remove and discard the stem and seeds. Cover the chilies in boiling water and let soften for 5 minutes. In a blender or food processor, purée the chilies with enough soaking liquid to form a thick paste.

2 Heat the skillet again over medium-high heat, and then add the olive oil. Sauté the onion and garlic until translucent, about 3 minutes. Increase the heat and add the beef and 2 teaspoons of the salt. Brown the beef, stirring occasionally to pick up browned bits on the bottom of the pan as the moisture evaporates, about 15 minutes. If the meat is excessively fatty (your judgment call), spoon off some of the fat, but leave some for flavor.

3 Stir in the cumin and cook for 30 seconds. Add the chili paste, red pepper flakes, oregano, bay leaf, jalapeños, and the remaining teaspoon of salt. Stir to combine well.

4 Add the tomatoes and beer and simmer for 30 minutes. Add the beans and cook for an additional 20 minutes. Add water if needed for desired consistency. Serve with preferred condiments (see headnote). ✳

meatballs and tomato sauce

makes 30 1½-inch meatballs

Meatballs in our family are no laughing matter. One set of my father's Italian grandparents insisted that formed pork meatballs be dropped into a simmering sauce to cook. The other set insisted that the meatballs be fried first and then added to the sauce. My non-Italian mom brought her own refinements to the controversy, making baked mini meatball sandwiches, but she still used only pork meat for her version, never beef. My husband and I are the ones who introduced beef into the mix. Whatever your preference, start with 2 pounds of ground meat for this recipe. What type of meat is up to you: all beef, half beef/half pork, part veal. If spaghetti and meatballs are for dinner, you'd better have made enough for seconds, late-night raids, and leftovers. They freeze beautifully in the sauce.

Parmesan cheese can be substituted for the Pecorino Romano, but the Romano brings a more pungent flavor.

⅓ cup milk

2 slices best-quality bread, crusts removed

1 pound ground pork

1 pound ground beef

2 garlic cloves, minced

2 tablespoons minced onion

2 large eggs, lightly beaten

¾ cup grated Pecorino Romano cheese, plus more for serving

2 tablespoons chopped fresh parsley leaves

¼ teaspoon freshly ground black pepper

½ teaspoon coarse salt (use 1 teaspoon if Parmesan is substituted for the Romano)

2 tablespoons extra-virgin olive oil

2 28-ounce cans best-quality whole tomatoes, pulsed with juices in a blender

Freshly grated Parmesan cheese, for serving (optional)

1 In a small saucepan, heat the milk. Soak the bread in the milk, turning the slices over to absorb it. Cool and mince the bread. Place it in a large bowl. Add the meats, garlic, onion, eggs, cheese, parsley, pepper, and salt. Using clean hands, mix together until completely combined.

2 Have a rimmed baking sheet or platter ready. If you have time, chill the raw meatballs to firm them up. Roll into 1½-inch meatballs. (If you periodically run cold water over your hands, the meat won't stick to them as you roll.)

3 Heat a 14-inch skillet (or two smaller skillets to fry in batches) over high heat. Add the olive oil and when it is very hot, add the meatballs in a single layer. Don't crowd the pan; work in batches if necessary. Fry the meatballs without moving for a few minutes, then turn as they cook to brown on all sides, 8 to 10 minutes. Spoon out any excess oil from the pan, carefully scraping around the meatballs.

4 Add the tomatoes and scrape the bottom of the pan to incorporate all the browned bits. Simmer for 30 minutes. Serve hot pasta with 3 meatballs on top, some sauce, the grated cheese, and freshly ground black pepper. ✴

Meatball Heroes A large pot of hot meatballs in sauce will also make for some hearty sandwiches. Buy hero rolls; heat and slice. Halve the meatballs and tuck inside the roll. Top with grated cheese or sliced mozzarella, then broil for a minute to melt.

Meat Loaf For a fantastic meat loaf twist, add ⅓ pound of minced mortadella or a flavorful bologna to this recipe. Form the whole mixture into a free-form loaf in a large baking dish, coat in bread crumbs, drizzle with olive oil, and bake in a 400°F oven for 45 minutes.

basic beef stew

serves 10 to 12, or 6 for one meal, with leftovers to freeze for another

Achieving a deep rich flavor in a basic beef stew depends upon browning the meat. It takes a little extra time and attention so why not double your efforts and prepare enough to feed a large crowd, or freeze half the batch for another meal. Once the dark golden sear is achieved on the meat and the aromatics are sautéed, the stew simmers away unattended on the stove. I serve the stew over buttered egg noodles or rice.

5 large carrots, peeled, 2 finely diced and 3 cut into ¾-inch chunks

4 celery stalks, peeled (2 finely diced, 2 sliced crosswise into ¼-inch slices)

6 medium potatoes, peeled and cut into 1½-inch chunks

4 pounds beef, cut into 2-inch chunks (use chuck steak or half chuck/half bottom round)

Coarse salt and freshly ground black pepper

2 tablespoons vegetable oil

¼ cup all-purpose flour, for dredging

1 tablespoon unsalted butter

2 onions, chopped

4 garlic cloves, minced

2 tablespoons tomato paste

3 sprigs of fresh thyme, or 1½ teaspoons dried thyme

½ cup red wine (optional)

8 cups beef or chicken broth

1 tablespoon hot red pepper sauce (optional)

1 Float the carrot chunks, celery slices, and potato chunks in a large bowl of cold water until needed.

2 Toss the meat with a generous amount of salt and pepper. Heat a large Dutch oven or other heavy-bottomed pot over medium-high heat. Swirl the oil into the pot. Working in batches, coat the meat pieces in flour, and add to the pot. Brown on all sides, about 8 to 10 minutes, then transfer the browned meat to a plate. Repeat until all the meat is browned, adding more oil if necessary.

3 Pour off all but a few tablespoons of fat. Swirl in the butter. Add the onions, garlic, diced carrots, and diced celery. Cook on medium-low heat until lightly caramelized, 10 to 12 minutes. Stir in the tomato paste and the thyme and cook for 2 more minutes.

4 Raise the heat to high. Add the wine, if using (or ½ cup of broth), and stir to deglaze the pan, scraping up the browned bits stuck to the bottom. Return the meat to the pan and add the broth, which should cover the meat (add water if necessary). Bring to a boil, then reduce the heat to low, cover, and simmer for 2 hours.

5 Drain the carrots, celery, and potato chunks. Add to the pot and cook until tender, 30 to 35 minutes. Remove 4 potato pieces, then mash them and stir back into the stew to slightly thicken the mixture. Stir in the hot sauce, if using. Taste and add more salt if necessary. Serve hot. (To freeze: Cool the stew and store in an airtight plastic container in the freezer for up to 3 months.) *

Browning Meat The mantra: Don't crowd the pan. Make sure your pan is very hot before you add the (preferably room-temperature) meat pieces; leave enough room surrounding each piece in the pan so air can circulate around the meat as it browns. Don't move the pieces for a few minutes as the sear sets in. Turn and repeat the process on all sides of the meat. It's the browned bits on the bottom of the pan, known as the "fond," that forms the basis for the flavor of the stewy sauce. If you crowd the pieces together in the pan, the meat will steam as all the liquid releases instead of browning.

Slow Cookers This electric cooking appliance, which permits food to cook safely at a steady low temperature, unattended, is an invaluable tool for busy families who enjoy eating stews, braises, or pot roasts. Strategic planning of shopping and timing is all that's required to make a slow cooker yield regular, delicious meals.

roast leg of lamb with lemon, garlic, and oregano

serves 6 to 8

The ritual Easter meal in our house means this roast leg of lamb cooked for dinner with an abundance of side dishes, like Stuffed Artichokes (page 208), Spinach Feta Pocket Pies (page 66), and White Bean Salad (page 100). This recipe calls for first covering the lamb in a seasoning paste to keep it marinating for as long as possible, anywhere from one to twenty-four hours—the longer the better. (This is a fantastic paste to use on roast chicken, too.) The meat cooks beautifully both in the oven and on the grill. Slice leftovers for pita stuffed sandwiches topped with Tabbouleh Salad (page 90).

2 whole lemons, washed, seeded, and chopped

2 sprigs of fresh rosemary, leaves removed

5 to 6 garlic cloves, peeled

1 tablespoon coarse salt

½ teaspoon freshly ground black pepper

2 to 4 tablespoons extra-virgin olive oil

1 boneless leg of lamb, butterflied, boned, and cut to lay flat (about 5 pounds)

1 Place the chopped lemon, rosemary, garlic, salt, pepper, and olive oil in a food processor. A blender can also be used, if done in batches. If you have neither, finely chop all ingredients together.

2 Open up the lamb and lay it flat. Spread and massage the lemon paste evenly over the inside and outside of the lamb. Place in a baking dish and cover, or in a large resealable plastic bag. Refrigerate overnight to marinate, turning occasionally.

3 Preheat the oven to 450°F. Remove the meat from the refrigerator 30 to 60 minutes before cooking. Place the lamb on a rack in a foil-lined roasting pan or rimmed baking sheet. Place the meat in the oven and after 5 minutes, reduce the temperature to 425°F. Roast for 45 minutes, or until medium rare, 140°F on an instant-read thermometer. Allow the meat to rest for 10 to 15 minutes before carving and serving. ∗

Variation: Grilling the Lamb Prepare the fire for indirect cooking (see page 139). Place the meat, fat side up, on the side of the grill that is not over the coals. Cover the grill and open both the bottom and cover vents. Cook for 30 minutes. Turn the meat around to allow it to cook evenly; cover, and cook for another 30 minutes. As the fat melts on top, and the marinade paste begins to turn golden, press the paste into the meat with the back of your tongs. Cook until the internal temperature on an instant-read thermometer reaches 140°F.

papaya chutney

makes 3 cups

This chutney is an all-purpose condiment, delicious with roast lamb, grilled chicken, or sautéed pork chops. It offers a sensational and unexpected flavor combination—try it on a cheese plate or smear it on a sandwich with roast meat. Also, given its many uses and beautiful orange color, it makes a great gift.

3 medium papayas, peeled, seeded, and chopped (about 2 cups)

1 chayote, peeled, pitted, and diced, or 1 peeled and diced cucumber

½ green or red bell pepper, or a combination, finely chopped

¼ whole lime, diced

2 teaspoons ground ginger or minced peeled fresh ginger

3 teaspoons coarse salt

1 cup white vinegar

1½ cups sugar

¾ cup water

1 Place all ingredients in a medium saucepan and cook gently over low heat for 2 hours, stirring periodically.

2 Remove from the heat, and allow the chutney to cool. Store in glass jars in the refrigerator for up to 6 months. *

Grilled lamb chops with Papaya Chutney

A Menu for a
Twenty-first Birthday Party

The idea for the party came together rather spontaneously. Since no formal invitations had been sent, I hadn't a clue how many people would show up or how many could fit in our small apartment. But on January 8, 2008, the temperature soared to seventy degrees in New York City, so I set up the bar outside on the terrace, and inside I laid out a buffet that could be nibbled on all night. I figured most guests just wanted to party.

Anticipating our firstborn son's twenty-first birthday party filled me with great pleasure, both as a mother and as a mother who is a caterer at heart. I allowed three days, around the edges of everyday life, to cook the birthday meal and to avoid stress and last-minute fumbling. Strategic menu planning, shopping, and prep were key, as was the decision to make an abundance of a few select dishes rather than too little of many. I admit that the libation liberation of a legal drinking age helped, too. So I offered a spicy punch.

If you're a pork lover, this would have been your night. I served two enormous pork shoulders cooked in different styles, along with several sheets of focaccia. Aside from one vegan guest and a few kosher friends, the group devoured the food. For drinks, we decided on a champagne toast, two versions of Scotchie Citrus Punch (one soft and one spiked; page 160), and cases of canned Mexican beer. Two kinds of cupcakes—lemon curd–filled vanilla with buttercream and mocha-frosted chocolate—stood in for a cake, allowing guests to eat their dessert right from the start of the party if they so chose.

For thirty guests over the course of five hours, the food and drink bill was under five hundred dollars.

cuban-style pork roast

serves 6 to 8 as a dinner roast

This dish will feed as many as ten people, and at $2.49 per pound, for a total of $18, it's really inexpensive. The meat cooks low and slow and needs very little attention. Here's a quick trick for big flavor: blend unpeeled, seeded pieces of citrus as a foundation for a seasoning paste. You can rub this paste all over any meat and marinate for several hours before cooking. I serve it with lots of rice, boiled yucca or potatoes, and some greens.

10 garlic cloves, peeled

4 tablespoons fresh oregano leaves (from about 5 sprigs), or 2 teaspoons dried oregano

4 tablespoons extra-virgin olive oil

3 whole limes, cut in pieces

1 tablespoon coarse salt

1 7½-pound boneless pork shoulder (also known as pork butt or picnic shoulder)

1 Purée the garlic, oregano, olive oil, limes, and salt in a blender or food processor.

2 Place the meat in a roasting pan, and score the fat on top of the pork. Rub the garlic mixture all over the pork. Cover and refrigerate overnight or up to 24 hours. Flip the roast occasionally and redistribute the rub.

3 Preheat the oven to 250°F. Remove the meat from the refrigerator 30 minutes before cooking. Place the pan in the oven, fat side up, and add 1 cup of water to the pan. Roast, uncovered, occasionally basting the meat with juices and rub and turning the pan to promote even cooking. Cook for 6 to 8 hours, until the meat easily shreds. Let rest for 15 minutes, then shred and serve. *

CUBAN SANDWICHES FOR A CROWD

Thinly slice the pork. Slice open baguettes. Spread one side with mustard and mayonnaise. Layer on pork, sliced ham, and Swiss cheese. Spread the other side with the pan drippings and close the sandwich. Wrap the sandwiches in foil, then weight down with pans, cans, bricks, or books. When ready to serve, warm in 200°F oven for 30 minutes. Unwrap, then slice into individual sandwiches. This recipe yields enough pork for 4 baguettes, or 16 pieces.

scotchie citrus punch

makes 6 cocktails

Over the years I've discovered that feeding and nurturing boys and men requires periodically rejuvenating yourself. While visiting Jamaican friends, we created this unbelievable cocktail by turning to the spice cabinet and fruit and vegetable larder for inspiration. Made with local Jamaican allspice, citrus, and hot scotch bonnet peppers, it was aptly named a Scotchie, both in honor of the pepper and the mixologist. I always make half of the batch "soft," without rum.

1 cup natural sugar, less if no unsweetened citrus such as lime is used

1 cup freshly squeezed citrus juice (grapefruit, orange, lime or any combo that isn't too sweet)

1 tablespoon fresh ginger, peeled and thinly sliced

2 whole scotch bonnet or habanero peppers

8 whole allspice

Ice

Appleton Estate Jamaican Rum

Club soda

Slices of fresh lime

Combine the sugar, citrus juice, ginger, peppers, and allspice in a small pan and bring to a boil. Cool and strain the mixture. Fill 6 glasses with ice. Fill each glass halfway with the citrus mixture, add 1 shot of rum each, top with club soda, and stir. Garnish with a slice of lime and serve. *

**TO SERVE 30 GUESTS,
HERE ARE THE QUANTITIES:**

8 cups sugar

20 cups (1 gallon) citrus juice

20 tablespoons sliced fresh ginger

19 whole scotch bonnet peppers

Scant ¼ cup whole allspice

1 1.5-liter bottle (or 2 750-ml bottles) rum

2 liters club soda

When I make a large batch, I make and store the mix without club soda, adding the fizzy stuff only when ready to serve. *

asian-style pork roast

serves 8 to 10 as an entrée or 25 as part of a buffet

The idea for it comes from a New York City restaurant at which a whole pork shoulder is shared around a common table.

One preorders a large pork butt, which is placed in the center of the table with all the "Bo Ssam" fixings for a large group to enjoy. Done at home, this recipe requires long, slow cooking until the tender pork is easy to shred. The meat is served with its own juices directly from the pan. Alongside are washed and dried soft lettuce cups and whatever fixings you like: fresh cilantro, chilies, or chopped scallions are perfect. I boil down the extra marinade until it has a syrupy consistency and serve that too, along with white rice or bread to sop up every last bit of gooey drippings. At the tail end of our last party, not a scrap of meat remained. We resorted to drizzling the last bit of sauce over squares of defrosted sandwich bread.

2 cups honey

10 ounces soy sauce

¼ cup sambal chili paste

¼ cup shaoxing cooking wine or dry sherry

½ cup peeled fresh ginger, coarsely chopped

2 whole star anise (about 10 petals)

1 9-pound boneless pork shoulder (10 to 11 pounds with bone)

2 heads of Bibb lettuce, leaves cleaned and left whole

10 scallions, sliced in quarters

1 bunch of cilantro, cleaned and stems removed

1 Purée the honey, soy sauce, chili paste, wine, ginger, and star anise in a blender or food processor.

2 Place the pork in a large roasting pan and pour over enough marinade to cover, reserving whatever doesn't fit. Boil down the extra to serve as a sauce. Cover and refrigerate overnight, or up to 24 hours. Occasionally turn the meat and redistribute the marinade.

3 Preheat the oven to 250°F. Remove the meat from the refrigerator 30 minutes prior to roasting.

4 Roast the meat, skin side up, in the marinade until it will easily shred with a fork, 6 to 8 hours; occasionally baste the meat with the marinade and turn the pan for even cooking.

5 Serve the pork shredded in the pan with scallions and cilantro on the side, using whole lettuce leaves for wrapping. ✶

Pork Shoulder Pork shoulder, also known as pork butt or picnic shoulder, is without a doubt the most economical cut of meat you can get to feed a family, whether cooking it with or without the bone. If your recipe calls for a boneless shoulder, as this one does, ask the butcher to remove the bone (save to flavor beans) or remove it yourself: use a thin sharp knife to slice the blade along all the sides of the bone to remove.

pork chops with apples and onions

serves 6

This simple dish was one of the first my eldest son requested the recipe for when he got his own kitchen. It's easy to vary: Sometimes we replace the onions with leeks or add a sliced potato, and we have deglazed the pan with beer, white wine, chicken broth, or water. Soft sweet apples and savory onions combine with the salty pork for a tastiness that never disappoints. A big pot of rice, a couple of vegetables, and you have a generous and filling dinner.

6 bone-in pork chops (loin or shoulder), cut ¾ inch thick

Coarse salt and freshly ground black pepper

1 tablespoon extra-virgin olive oil or vegetable oil

2 tablespoons unsalted butter

1 large white onion, sliced

2 to 3 apples, cored and sliced (about 3 cups)

1 cup beer, white wine, cider, or chicken broth

1 Trim the chops of excess fat. Sprinkle generously with salt and pepper on both sides. Heat a 14-inch cast-iron skillet (if you have a smaller one, you'll need to work in batches) over high heat, and then swirl in the olive oil. Lay in the pork chops and don't move them for a few minutes, to assure a good golden sear forms. Turn and brown well on the second side for a total of about 10 minutes. Remove the chops to a warm plate.

2 Swirl the butter into the pan. Add the onion and apples. Sauté until the onion slices are lightly caramelized and the apples have begun to soften, about 8 minutes. Stir in the beer or other liquid. Return the chops to the pan.

3 Cook until the pork is tender, about 15 more minutes (depending on the size of the chops), turning halfway through and covering the chops with the apple mixture. If the apple mixture needs a little thickening, remove the chops to the warm plate again and simmer the mixture on high for a few minutes to reduce. Serve the chops over rice or mashed potatoes with a large spoonful of the apple-onion mixture over the top. ✳

richie's grilled baby back ribs

serves 4

Ribs are a most beloved meal, but it seems like you can never make enough when the whole crew is together. This recipe is cooked on a grill, but if you're cooking the ribs in the oven (see below), you'll need to add more seasoning to assure an authentic taste; to approximate the deep flavor of barbecue smoke, add one tablespoon each of cocoa and instant coffee to the rub. You can serve your favorite homemade or store-bought barbecue sauce on the side, although these ribs are so tasty when cooked properly that no sauce is needed.

2 racks baby back ribs (4 pounds total) or pork spareribs

Coarse salt and freshly ground black pepper

2 teaspoons sweet paprika

½ teaspoon smoked Spanish paprika (if available)

1 teaspoon dried sage

½ teaspoon ground cinnamon

½ teaspoon ground cumin

¼ teaspoon cayenne pepper

2 tablespoons granulated brown sugar

1 cup favorite barbecue sauce

1 Sprinkle the ribs generously with salt and black pepper. In a small bowl, combine the sweet and smoked paprikas, sage, cinnamon, cumin, cayenne, and brown sugar. Rub the mixture into the meat and let stand at room temperature for at least 30 minutes or refrigerated for up to 2 hours.

2 Prepare a charcoal grill for indirect heat. (If oven-roasting, see below.)

3 Place the ribs on the grill, on very low heat, 250°F or less. Remember, don't cook ribs over direct flames. Cover and almost close the vents. Every 20 minutes, turn the ribs around to cook evenly. They should be perfectly cooked within 1½ to 2 hours; if using pork spareribs, cook an additional half an hour. Serve with barbecue sauce on the side. *

Make Homemade Rub Our simple flavorful rub, with its balance of salt, sweet, and spice, is practically effortless and won't leave the unpleasant chemical aftertaste associated with many commercial versions.

Oven-Roasting as an Alternative Place rub-seasoned ribs on a baking sheet and cook for 1½ to 2 hours at 350°F. Increase the heat to 425°F, brush over barbecue sauce, and cook for 15 more minutes until caramelized.

glazed ham

serves 8, with generous leftovers

A good ham is not only a special choice for a holiday meal, it's also a bargain choice for everyday meals, especially when you're feeding boys. A premium ten-pound ham, at about forty dollars, feeds at least eight people. It provides leftovers to slice with the next morning's eggs and sandwiches for lunch, and there's enough to add to the red beans and rice (see page 188) for yet another meal.

All hams aren't created equal. I like one that isn't too salty; an applewood smoke is milder than a hickory. Purchase the best you can find, and trial and error will lead you to a favorite brand. What's your preference? Glazes are endless. I like one with a flavor balance of sweet, tart, and spicy mixed with a hint of alcohol, such as apricot mustard, orange molasses, or maple syrup pepper. Use this recipe as a guide, switching out the brown sugar and rum for other similar ingredients to suit your taste.

1 10-pound cured and smoked ham (preferably bone-in)

¾ cup brown sugar

¼ cup plus 1 tablespoon Dijon, grainy, or Bavarian-style mustard (or a combination)

¼ cup golden rum

2 tablespoons white wine vinegar

1 Preheat the oven to 325°F. Remove the ham from the packaging and score the fat all over in a diamond pattern with a sharp knife. Wrap the ham in foil, bone down, and place it on a rimmed baking sheet. Bake for 45 minutes.

2 Meanwhile, place the sugar, mustard, rum, and vinegar in a small saucepan and bring to a boil, dissolving the sugar. Unwrap the ham and brush half of the glaze all over it. Bake, unwrapped, for 15 minutes while increasing the heat to 400°F. Bake for an additional 20 minutes. Brush on the remaining glaze and bake for 15 to 20 more minutes, or until the glaze is caramelized. Let the ham rest before carving. *

Scoring Shallow lines are cut on the surface of the meat, often in a diamond pattern, both to embed the flavor of a glaze and to permit the fat to drain and crisp.

Boys' Winter Break

Two working parents and three active boys often make for crazy scheduling challenges. More often than not, a school vacation creeps up with no plans in place. All you need is one unoccupied boy at home for a week to drive everyone, including himself, insane. One winter break we pulled together a last-minute three-day ski trip for our youngest son and his friend and me. I rented lodgings with a kitchen near the slopes, preplanned meals (even lunch was eaten in), and did our grocery shopping before leaving home.

Have you ever tried to affordably feed several meals a day to ravenous boys captive at a ski resort? The prices are too high and the quality of the food is too low. For this trip, our grocery bill for eight meals, plus snacks and drinks, serving two growing boys and one adult, was under two hundred dollars. We could have even served a couple more boys at each meal; we returned home with enough extra groceries for a few more dinners. I bought all the food at home (with some staples pilfered from our kitchen pantry) and packed it up in a large cooler: heavy cans, bottles, and boxes in the bottom of several heavy canvas bags, with everything else on top. A smaller, soft to-go cooler traveled between the boys in the backseat of the car for lunch and quick snacks. Meals were made on-site in a small but serviceable kitchen.

Menus for a Winter Trip

MONDAY

BREAKFAST
Breakfast Burrito (page 23)
Hot chocolate (page 59)

LUNCH TO GO
Italian Pressed Sandwiches (page 75)
Clementines

DINNER
Chicken and Dumplings (page 125)
Green salad with Green Goddess Ranch
     Salad Dressing (page 98)
Crisp Toffee Chocolate Bars (page 251)

TUESDAY

BREAKFAST
Grapefruit with honey
Pear-Stuffed French Toast (page 42)
Oven-Fried Bacon (page 45)
Date tea

LUNCH
Oxtail Broth with Noodles or other
     faux ramen (page 82)
Cold spinach salad
Spiced Chai Latte (page 58)

DINNER
Green salad
Luscious Oven-Braised Short Ribs
     (page 143) with potatoes

WEDNESDAY

BREAKFAST
Frosty Banana Berry Smoothie
     (page 52)
Old-Fashioned Pancakes (page 37)
Maple-glazed bacon

LUNCH TO GO
Chicken Salad Sandwich (page 78)
Carrot and celery sticks
Apples and oranges

**SNACKS (FOR THE AFTERNOON
AND THE CAR RIDE)**
Cheesy Corn Snack (page 110)
Iced Sweet Rooibos Tea (page 54)
Crisp Toffee Chocolate Bars (page 251)
Fruit

broiled or grilled salmon teriyaki

serves 6

Broiling or grilling melds and caramelizes the soy-sweet flavor of teriyaki with the salmon's oils and provides a familiar flavor to help get non-fish-eaters interested in fish. I remove the skin before serving it to the kids to make it more appealing, but, if I'm grilling, I do serve the crispy skin separately, for those who want it. This recipe works equally well with different fish, but the cooking time will change. Generally plan on 8 minutes cooking per inch (thickness) of boneless fish.

1 cup soy sauce

¼ cup honey

2 tablespoons fresh lemon juice or mild vinegar

1 inch of peeled fresh ginger, sliced

3 garlic cloves, smashed

2 pounds boneless salmon fillet, pin bones removed

1 Whisk the soy, honey, and lemon juice together in a large enough dish to fit the salmon. Stir in the ginger and garlic. Place the salmon, skin side up, in the sauce and marinate for at least 10 minutes or up to 30 minutes.

2 Preheat a broiler or prepare coals to very hot in a grill. Remove the salmon from the marinade, pat it dry with paper towels, and place it skin side down on an oiled pan or grill grate. Cook until it is slightly firm to the touch, 10 to 15 minutes, depending on thickness. While the salmon is cooking, brush it a couple of times with the marinade to use it all up. Immediately remove the skin while the fish is hot. Serve. *

BUYING FRESH, SUSTAINABLE FISH

I buy wild Alaskan salmon because I prefer its flavor and its firmer texture and current sustainability. It's much more expensive than the farmed alternative, however, so I buy it less frequently and use the freshest available fish instead. Befriend your fishmonger and you'll acquire the information you need to choose high-quality fresh seafood and receive guidance for the best available choice at that time. You can also check www.seafoodwatch.com to help you make responsible decisions or check the Environmental Defense Fund (www.edf.org), which provides lists of eco-best fish and alternatives.

broiled lemon-pepper striped bass

serves 1

My second son always loved the kitchen. Eventually he began working at a fish restaurant and started eating fish all the time, every which way—a very un-boy-like practice, you might think. One day he asked for fish, so I bought two varieties in single portions. He asked for one with a soy glaze, and one with brown butter. "Huh?" I said. "Not here, honey, this isn't Le Bernardin." The fewest ingredients for the biggest flavor are what I was going for, what he calls my "simple, rustic style." Meanwhile, he cooks for us now!

1 lemon, cut in half
(zest one half and reserve the other
for garnish)

¼ teaspoon cracked black pepper

1 6-ounce piece of wild striped bass fillet

Extra-virgin olive oil for drizzling

Coarse salt

1 Preheat the broiler and slide in a small ovenproof pan to heat as well.

2 Mince together the lemon zest and pepper on a cutting board. Rub the fish with the olive oil. Sprinkle with salt. Rub the lemon pepper all over the top of the fish. Drizzle over more olive oil, place on the preheated pan, and broil for 6 minutes. Serve with a lemon wedges. *

Fish Fillet or Steak?
A fish fillet is the boneless meat sliced vertically off the bone, on both sides. While the fillet is easier to cook than a steak and perhaps is more visually appealing, a fish steak, cut horizontally across the bone, takes added flavor from the bone. Also, the bone helps to hold the delicate flesh together, making it a good choice for barbecuing.

seared soy-sesame arctic char

serves 1

Arctic char, a tasty fish with beautiful melon-colored flesh, can substitute for brook trout, Tasmanian ocean trout, or even salmon, but it's an excellent choice of fish to eat as it is presently sustainable (see page 169).

1 tablespoon soy sauce

1 teaspoon honey

¼ teaspoon toasted sesame oil

1 6-ounce piece of arctic char

Coarse salt and freshly ground black pepper

1 In a small bowl, stir together the soy sauce, honey, and sesame oil. Season the fish with salt and pepper and brush with half of the sauce.

2 Heat a small cast-iron skillet over high heat. Sear the fish skin side up for 4 minutes. Pour the remaining sauce over the fish and swirl the sauce around the pan. Carefully turn the fish, spoon the sauce over the top, and cook for 3 more minutes, until the fish is just cooked through. Serve immediately. *

shrimp scampi

serves 6

This dish can be served with crusty bread or over rice, or, as here, dished up with pasta such as conghiglie rigate (shells). Serve small shrimp with toothpicks, and you'll have a delicious appetizer. For many shrimp dishes I leave the shell on, which intensifies the flavor but makes for messy eating. In this recipe, though, the shrimp definitely needs to be shelled and deveined.

1 pound pasta, or 3 cups cooked rice

Coarse salt

2 tablespoons extra-virgin olive oil, plus more for drizzling

2 pounds large shrimp, peeled and deveined

Freshly ground black pepper

5 garlic cloves, minced

½ teaspoon crushed red pepper flakes, plus more for garnish

1½ tablespoons freshly grated lemon zest

¼ cup white wine

Juice of 1 lemon

¼ cup chopped fresh parsley leaves

1. Bring a large pot of water to a boil over high heat. Add the pasta and a generous pinch of salt and cook until al dente. Drain the pasta, reserving ½ cup of the pasta water.

2. Meanwhile, heat a large sauté pan over high heat. Add 1½ tablespoons of the oil and swirl it to coat the pan. Add the shrimp in a single layer. Sprinkle with salt and pepper. After 2 minutes, turn the shrimp over; add the remaining 1½ teaspoons of oil, the garlic, and the red pepper flakes. Stir constantly for 1 to 2 minutes, regulating the heat to avoid burning the garlic.

3. Add the lemon zest and white wine to the shrimp. Stir to reduce the wine slightly. Add the lemon juice, cooked pasta, and reserved pasta water to the pan. Toss to combine. Remove from the heat and sprinkle with the parsley. Serve with a drizzle of olive oil and extra red pepper flakes on each serving. *

pasta alla checca

serves 4 generously

I learned to make this easy and classic *alla checca* sauce in Italy. The freshest tomatoes with all their juices are the whole thrust of this dish. You can make the sauce early on the day you plan to serve it—just combine all the ingredients in your serving bowl and let them meld together. Or, do so at least an hour before the cooked pasta is tossed right in the bowl. You can serve this dish hot or at room temperature.

1 pound tomatoes (3 to 5 medium), cored

⅓ cup extra-virgin olive oil

4 garlic cloves, smashed

2 teaspoons dried oregano, or 1 tablespoon fresh oregano leaves

1 cup packed fresh basil leaves, torn

1 teaspoon coarse salt, plus more for the pasta

¼ teaspoon crushed red pepper flakes

1 pound spaghetti or other pasta

Freshly grated Parmesan cheese, for serving

1 Rip the tomatoes into small pieces and place in a large pasta or other serving bowl. Pour in the olive oil. Add the garlic, oregano, basil, salt, and red pepper flakes.

2 Stir all the ingredients together to combine. Let the mixture marinate, covered, at room temperature for at least 1 hour and up to 8 hours.

3 Bring a large pot of water to a boil. Add the pasta and a generous pinch of salt and cook for 2 minutes short of the package instructions; you want it to be al dente (firm but tender). Do not overcook.

4 Drain the pasta and transfer directly into the sauce. Toss to combine. Remove garlic, if desired. Serve with grated cheese to top each portion. ∗

CHEESE VARIATION

Mozzarella can be added to this dish at the same time the hot pasta is tossed with the sauce. The trick is to cube and freeze the cheese 30 minutes in advance. The chill will allow the cheese to be tossed into the hot pasta without it melting too fast as it softens.

spaghetti bolognese

serves 4 to 6

One day, when I found I didn't have time to make a traditional Bolognese sauce, I came up with this abbreviated version of the original. I wanted that meaty-vegetably flavor and unctuous texture without the typical long cooking time—and I got it! It worked out very well and has been made over and over again ever since. Spaghetti goes well with this meat sauce, but just about any pasta you have in the cupboard will do nicely.

1 tablespoon extra-virgin olive oil

½ onion, finely diced (½ cup)

1 carrot, finely diced

2 celery stalks, finely diced

4 ounces pancetta, finely diced (optional)

1 pound ground beef, or a combination of beef and pork

Coarse salt

½ cup red or white wine

1 28-ounce can best-quality tomatoes, pulsed in a blender

½ cup cream or milk

Freshly ground black pepper

¼ teaspoon crushed red pepper flakes

1 pound spaghetti or other pasta

1½ tablespoons unsalted butter

½ cup freshly grated Parmesan cheese

1 Heat a saucepan over low heat. Add the olive oil, onion, carrot, and celery and sauté over low heat until lightly caramelized, about 12 minutes. Add the pancetta and beef and cook, separating the meat into small pieces, until browned, 10 to 15 minutes. Drain off most of the fat. Stir in 1 teaspoon salt.

2 Pour the wine into the beef mixture to deglaze the pan; stir to loosen the browned bits on the bottom of the pan. Cook for about 2 minutes, until the wine is almost evaporated. Add the tomatoes and stir in the cream, black pepper, and red pepper flakes. Gently simmer for about 40 minutes, until the sauce has reduced and thickened.

3 Start cooking the spaghetti when the sauce is within 10 minutes of being done. Bring a large pot of water to a boil over high heat. Add the spaghetti and a generous pinch of salt to the boiling water and cook until al dente, about 8 minutes. Drain.

4 Stir the butter into the bolognese sauce and season to taste with salt and pepper. Spoon the sauce over the pasta and serve with grated Parmesan cheese on top. ∗

lasagna

makes 12 manly servings

On the trail of the boy-perfect lasagna, we've learned a few tricks: Start with a thick tomato sauce and allow the lasagna to set after cooking, so it will cut into clean, compact slices. Boil noodles only half as long as the package directs, because mushy equals airline lasagna. Pecorino Romano cheese offers more punch than Parmesan, and the sausage needs a crisp crust. This lasagna feeds five or six for dinner, including seconds, and is still delicious reheated the next day. Stash it in the freezer and you'll never be left unprepared to feed a mass of guys. It goes straight from freezer to oven, but add twenty minutes to the cooking time.

1 pound lasagna noodles or packaged precooked lasagna noodles

Coarse salt

5 links sweet Italian sausage, or a mixture of hot and sweet, pierced with a fork

1 large egg

1 pound ricotta cheese

¾ cup freshly grated Pecorino Romano or Parmesan cheese, plus more for serving

5 cups Basic Italian Tomato Sauce (see page 179; double the recipe and cook for 30 minutes longer to thicken)

1 pound fresh or prepackaged mozzarella cheese, cut crosswise into ⅓-inch-thick slices

Extra-virgin olive oil, for drizzling

1 Bring a large pot of water to a boil over high heat. Add the noodles and a generous pinch of salt and cook for half as long as the package suggests. Drain and float in cold water. (Skip this step if noodles are precooked.)

2 Preheat the oven to 350°F. In a medium skillet over medium-high heat, fry the sausage links until cooked through, about 10 minutes. With kitchen scissors, cut the sausage into disks in the pan and continue to fry over low heat until the cut surfaces are crispy, about 20 minutes. Drain off the fat.

3 In a medium bowl, stir together the egg, ricotta, and ½ cup of the Pecorino.

4 To assemble the lasagna, spread 1 cup of the tomato sauce in the bottom of a greased 9 x 13-inch baking dish. Drain and pat dry the noodles. Overlap one third of the noodles atop the sauce to cover the pan bottom. Spread all the cooked sausage over the noodles and spoon over another cup of sauce. Lay down the second third of noodles. Evenly dollop all the ricotta mixture on top of the noodles and flatten with the spoon to make an even layer. Top with the remaining noodles to completely cover the cheese. Pour over 1½ to 2 cups sauce to cover. Evenly lay all the mozzarella slices on top. Sprinkle around the remaining ¼ cup Pecorino and drizzle with olive oil.

5 Bake uncovered for 40 minutes, or until the lasagna is bubbling all over and lightly golden on top. Let rest for 10 to 15 minutes before slicing. Serve with grated cheese and warmed extra sauce at the table. ✴

tuna tomato pasta

serves 4 to 6

This is my oldest son's go-to dish when there is supposedly nothing left in the house to cook—meaning that if you have a well-stocked pantry, you can get a meal ready in minutes without having to shop. Always have a few "pantry recipes" like this up your sleeve.

1 tablespoon extra-virgin olive oil, plus more for drizzling

1 small onion, finely chopped

2 garlic cloves, minced

Pinch of crushed red pepper flakes, plus more for garnish

3 cans tuna, well drained

2 cans crushed tomatoes, with juice

Coarse salt and freshly ground black pepper

1 tablespoon chopped fresh oregano, thyme, or rosemary

1 pound penne or fusilli pasta

1 Bring a large pot of water to a boil over high heat.

2 Heat a medium saucepan and add the olive oil, swirling to coat the pan. Sauté the onion and garlic until the onion is translucent, about 5 minutes. Stir in the red pepper flakes. Add the tuna and stir, being careful not to break up the chunks too much.

3 Stir in the tomatoes, season with salt and black pepper, bring to a boil, and reduce the heat to a simmer. Cook for 20 to 30 minutes. Add the chopped herb a few minutes before serving.

4 While the sauce is simmering, cook the pasta, drain, and toss with the sauce. Top with a drizzle of olive oil and an extra sprinkle of red pepper flakes. *

Fresh Garlic ● To peel: Whack the garlic clove with the heel of your hand or the side of a knife, to slightly flatten it. The peel will slip easily off. ● To mince: When you want the garlic to all but disappear in your dish, alternate chopping and pressing down (with some salt sprinkled in) with the flat edge of your knife until it is almost as fine as a paste. A garlic press will mash or crush the clove as well, but it can also separate the flesh from its precious oils.

basic italian tomato sauce

makes 3 cups; enough for 1 pound of pasta

I suppose my family would say that this sauce, doused over pasta of any kind, is our most basic comfort food; we probably cook and serve it more often than anything else in this book. Any time a tomato sauce is called for, this is the one I use. I add fresh basil if I have it on hand, and butter, swirled in at the end, if I want an extra-unctuous batch of sauce.

1½ tablespoons extra-virgin olive oil

2 garlic cloves, minced

⅛ teaspoon crushed red pepper flakes

1 28-ounce can best-quality tomatoes, pulsed in a blender

½ teaspoon coarse salt

1 sprig of fresh basil (optional)

1 tablespoon unsalted butter (optional)

1 Heat a medium saucepan over medium heat. Swirl around the olive oil to coat the pan and when the oil is hot, add the garlic and red pepper flakes. Stir constantly for 30 seconds, just long enough to release the garlic's fragrance and transform it slightly from its raw state. Don't cook it to golden.

2 Raise the heat to high and stir in the tomatoes and salt. Bring to a boil, reduce the heat, and simmer, uncovered, for 30 minutes. In the last 5 minutes of cooking, add the basil sprig, if using. Remove the basil before serving and swirl in the butter, if using. ＊

Fried Pasta The day after a meal of spaghetti tossed with tomato sauce, we fry the pasta into a crispy heap for an unusual meal! It works well with any leftover pasta. Heat a 10-inch cast-iron skillet over medium high, then add olive oil to coat the pan. Fill with leftover pasta and fry untouched to form a golden crust on the bottom. Turn the pasta to heat through and serve with grated cheese.

spaghetti carbonara

serves 4 to 6

Basically this recipe is nothing more than bacon and eggs with pasta, and many versions of it exist—some with the addition of cream and sometimes wine and parsley, too. This is the very first dinner ever cooked by our third-born son (when he was fourteen) for his friends. The verdict? "Mad good!"

1 pound spaghetti

½ pound bacon, sliced crosswise into ½-inch pieces

3 large eggs

1 cup grated Parmesan cheese, plus extra for serving (optional)

Freshly ground black pepper

1 Bring a large pot of water to a boil over high heat and cook the spaghetti. Meanwhile, in a large skillet, cook the bacon over medium-low heat until just crispy, 8 to 10 minutes. Skim off some of the fat. Drain the pasta, add to the bacon in the pan, and toss to combine.

2 Whisk together the eggs, cheese, and pepper in a small bowl. Pour into the pasta, and combine thoroughly. Serve immediately with extra grated cheese, if desired. ∗

CARBONARA VARIATIONS
You can do any or all of the following:
- Add a couple of peeled whole or crushed garlic cloves to the frying bacon and discard them when golden brown or when the flavor has permeated the bacon.
- Deglaze the cooked bacon with ¼ cup of white wine.
- Whisk a couple tablespoons of cream into the egg mixture.
- Scatter chopped fresh parsley over the top.

seafood paella

serves 4 to 6

One summer evening, after a week of cooking chowders (for my job), I was left with some fresh seafood and little desire to cook—until I remembered paella, a Spanish dish of saffron-scented rice, meat, and seafood that is prepared all in one pot. Making it gave me a chance to use linguiça, a delicious Portuguese sausage. It fed our hungry group with no more than a simple green salad and loaf of bread.

2 1½-pound lobsters

4½ teaspoons extra-virgin olive oil

1 small yellow onion, peeled and chopped

1 red bell pepper, cored, seeded, and diced

2 links linguiça (about ½ pound), skinned and chopped; or chopped cured Spanish-style chorizo or other cured sausage

2 cups white rice

3 cups fish or chicken broth, heated

1 pinch of crushed saffron

Coarse salt (depends on saltiness of linguiça and clams)

1 dozen littleneck clams, well cleaned

1½ pounds codfish or any firm-fleshed white fish, cut into 2-inch pieces

Sprigs of fresh parsley, coarsely chopped, for garnish

1 Bring 1½ inches of water to a boil in a large stockpot. Add the lobsters, cover, and cook for 13 minutes. Remove the lobsters and cool just enough to handle. Crack the shells and remove the meat. Keep the claws whole and chop the remainder of the meat into large pieces and reserve.

2 Preheat the oven to 450°F. Heat a 12-inch ovenproof skillet or paella pan over medium-high heat. Add the olive oil and sauté the onion and bell pepper until the onion is translucent, about 5 minutes. Add the linguiça and cook for 3 minutes. Gently stir in the rice and cook for a few minutes to lightly toast.

3 Add the broth, saffron, and salt, and bring to a boil over high heat. Remove from the heat and cover with a lid or with a sheet of foil and place the paella in the oven for 10 minutes. Uncover and scatter the clams around on top of the rice. Cover and cook for 15 minutes more, or until the clams are open and the liquid is absorbed. With 3 minutes left to cook, add the codfish and lobster. Discard any clams that do not open. Garnish with parsley and serve. ✷

thai-style fried rice

makes 1 large or 2 small servings

For years I made a basic Chinese-style quick-fried rice with soy sauce and eggs. But when I learned to make Thai fried rice from cookbook author Jeffrey Alford, it blew my mind; and I've made that version ever since. The trick is not to make it all at once.

If you are feeding a large group, get everything prepared and portioned out into servings before you start cooking. Fry it in small batches unless you have a couple of woks and another pair of hands to work beside you. Pressing the meat, rice, and seasoning into the pan really builds the flavor. This is a great use for the leftover rice sitting in the fridge. Use whatever extra vegetables you have on hand in place of the bok choy.

1 fresh green chili, sliced, or chili paste or crushed red pepper flakes

3 tablespoons fish sauce

2 tablespoons peanut oil or other vegetable oil (not olive oil)

2 garlic cloves, minced (1 tablespoon)

1 tablespoon minced peeled fresh ginger

2 scallions (both white and green parts), minced (about 3 tablespoons)

3 ounces boneless pork, such as shoulder or loin, cut into 2 x ½-inch strips

1½ cups cooked jasmine or basmati rice

1 cup shredded bok choy or other similar green vegetable

Sprigs of fresh cilantro, for garnish

½ cucumber, peeled and cubed

1 or 2 fresh lime wedges for garnish

1 Combine the chili and 2 tablespoons of the fish sauce in a small dipping bowl. Set aside. Heat a well-seasoned wok or frying pan over high heat. Add the oil and almost immediately add the garlic, ginger, and 2 tablespoons of scallions. Stir constantly for about 40 seconds. Be careful not to burn the mixture. Add the pork and continue to stir for 3 minutes, or until the pork is no longer pink.

2 Stir in the bok choy and cook until it is just tender, a couple of minutes. Stir in the cooked rice. Add the remaining tablespoon of fish sauce and stir to combine throughout the rice and heat through, about 2 minutes.

3 Serve immediately, garnished with cilantro, cucumber, the remaining tablespoon of scallion, and the lime. Serve the dipping sauce on the side. *

the freezer is your friend

I keep portion-sized packages of pork in the freezer so I can make this Thai-style Fried Rice at a moment's notice. With some strategic thinking, you can create a well-stocked freezer that will provide easy meals, especially when you think there is "nothing in the house." Make sure to clearly label and date each item before freezing.

- Slice and marinate portioned chicken, beef, or pork for a quick stir-fry.

- Stock tough-to-get fresh ingredients for specialty cooking—chilies, lemongrass, lime leaves, galangal—when you see them in the market.

- Make extra rice and freeze in 1-cup portions.

- Buy quality meat from known suppliers online or at farmers' markets. Wrap tightly and completely in plastic, label, and freeze.

- Buy extra bread at a premium bakery, cut it in portions, wrap it in plastic and foil, and freeze. (It'll defrost like fresh.) Even pre-sliced sandwich bread stays fresher than a loaf left too long on the counter or in the fridge.

- Make chicken stock when you have time and freeze in 1-cup portions for quick, healthful soups, stews, rice dishes, and sauces.

- Save leftover wine for those times when a recipe calls for only ½ cup of wine. Yes—it can be frozen!

- Make extra soup or stew and freeze for another meal.

- Keep bags of frozen berries for smoothies.

- Some frozen vegetables, such as peas and corn, are just fine for soups and sides. Freeze homegrown or farm-fresh vegetables by blanching them in boiling water, then placing them in ice water. Drain, then lay flat on a baking sheet, and place in the freezer until just frozen. Collect in resealable bags and squeeze air out. Seal and store for 3 to 4 months.

- Milk, butter, and juices all freeze well.

- Hard cheeses such as Parmesan and Pecorino Romano freeze well. Cut into 4-ounce pieces and wrap well.

- Make cookie dough, scoop it into balls, and freeze in a single layer on a baking sheet. Then collect them in a resealable plastic bag. Take out as few or as many as you want, defrost them on a baking sheet, and pop them in the oven for quick, hot homemade cookies.

paulbimbop
serves 6

Any time I hear praise about a man cooking, my ears perk up. Hearing that my colleague Jennifer's husband had created a family-style version of bibimbap, a delicious Korean rice dish, I longed to eat it and learn his tricks. Turns out Paul's Italian-Greek twist on a Korean recipe was as delicious as it sounded in the telling. Think of a pot of rice cooked with a golden, crunchy crust on the bottom, vegetables and meat mixed in, and eggs steamed on top. Paired with kimchi (a traditional seasoned and fermented vegetable condiment), this dish is addictive.

3 tablespoons extra-virgin olive oil

1 cup chopped onion

3 garlic cloves, minced

1½ pounds ground sirloin

1 teaspoon minced peeled fresh ginger

1 heaping tablespoon grainy mustard

1¼ cups chicken broth

½ pound cremini or button mushrooms, sliced

1 tablespoon fish sauce

1½ teaspoons soy sauce

½ teaspoon toasted sesame oil

Splash of rice vinegar

4 cups cooked rice, such as jasmine or basmati

1 pound bok choy or spinach, sliced 1 inch thick

7 ounces firm tofu, cubed

6 large eggs

4 to 5 scallions (both white and green parts), sliced, for garnishing

1 jar kimchi, for serving (optional)

1 Heat a large pot that has a tight-fitting lid over medium heat. Add the olive oil, onion, and garlic. After it begins cooking, add the meat, increase the heat, and cook for about 5 minutes, or stirring until the meat is browned. Add the ginger and mustard and continue cooking for 3 to 5 minutes, to caramelize the meat in the bottom of the pan.

2 Stir in the chicken broth. Add the mushrooms, fish sauce, soy sauce, and sesame oil. Splash in some vinegar.

3 Stir in the rice, bok choy, and tofu. Raise the heat to high. Smoothly tamp the mixture into the pan. Start listening for the "sizzling sound" as the rice crisps up in the bottom of the pan.

4 When the rice is heated through, make indentations in the top of the mixture for each egg and crack each one into a hole. Cover the pot and steam to cook the eggs, 2 to 3 minutes. To serve, scoop out a large spoonful of the mixture with an egg on top. Sprinkle with scallions. Serve with kimchi. ∗

spanish rice

serves 4 to 6

My mom's strategy for family cooking consisted of maybe a dozen recipes that she put into rotation and cooked most weeknights: roast pork, baked chicken, spaghetti, and hamburgers. One of my favorites was this "exotic" Spanish rice. My mother remembers hardly being able to get the meat browned without us kids practically spooning it all up before she could add the rice to the pan. What is curious is the name and how it found its way into the repertoire of a 1960s homemaker in Ontario, Canada. This is one of those cherished kinds of family dishes—simple and satisfying.

1 tablespoon extra-virgin olive oil

1 small onion, chopped

1 garlic clove, minced

½ green bell pepper, cored, seeded, and chopped (about ½ cup)

1 pound ground beef

2 teaspoons coarse salt

⅛ teaspoon freshly ground black pepper

1 14-ounce can tomatoes, drained and cut into small pieces (½ cup juice reserved)

1 cup long-grain white rice

1 cup water

1 Heat a 12-inch skillet over medium-high heat and swirl in the olive oil. Add the onion, garlic, and bell pepper. Reduce the heat to medium low and sauté the vegetables to soften, 2 to 3 minutes.

2 Add the beef, salt, and pepper. Increase the heat to high and cook until the meat is browned, 12 to 15 minutes.

3 Add the tomatoes, the reserved tomato juice, the rice, and the water. Stir just to combine, bring to a boil, and cover. Reduce the heat and simmer for 20 minutes, or until the liquid has been absorbed. Toss the mixture with a fork and serve immediately. *

In Praise of Moms

My mother is my role model for the healthful feeding of a family. At a time when frozen dinners and convenience food were pushed on homemakers, she doggedly stuck to preparing simple, fresh home-cooked meals day in and day out. It can't have been easy for our family of six with many strong opinions and requests.

basic white rice

makes 2 quarts

It may seem odd to include a recipe such as basic rice, but our family has actually spent years perfecting it. You can get it wrong too easily: soft and mushy or overly firm and tough. Rice preparation has many styles, depending on one's culture or usage. Our method is fast and reliable, a great method for the everyday cook. And it freezes well, too.

2 cups favorite long-grain white rice

1½ teaspoons coarse salt

3 cups water

1 Place the rice and salt in a medium saucepan. Add the water and briefly stir just to distribute evenly. Don't over-stir or you will release the starches and have gummy rice.

2 Bring to a rolling boil over high heat. Reduce the heat to the lowest possible temperature and cover the pot. Let the rice steam for at least 20 minutes, until it has absorbed all the water. It'll be fine if left a little longer, but avoid burning the bottom of the pan. Let the rice sit, covered, off the heat until ready to serve (up to 30 minutes). Fluff with a fork and serve. ✴

Leftover Rice Once you make the rice, you have the basis for: ● fried eggs on rice, a breakfast favorite ● quick fried rice ● a filler to dump into soups ● PaulBimbop (page 184) ● Rice pudding

new orleans—style red beans

serves 8

Childhood flavors and aromas have a potent hold over us all. My husband has talked endlessly about his mother's red beans and rice. It was a specialty of her hometown, New Orleans, and she served it weekly when he was a child. I've tried many different ways over the years to produce a version that approximates his flavor memory, but only after a recent trip to New Orleans, where I sampled different styles myself, did I succeed. This is one of the most economical meals to serve for a tableful of guys, and it can be further enhanced with a topping of your sausage of choice, split lengthwise and grilled (as on the facing page). Serve over the white rice with a bottle of hot sauce within reach.

1 tablespoon vegetable oil

1 small onion, finely chopped (about 1 cup)

2 celery stalks, peeled and finely chopped

½ red or green bell pepper, cored, seeded, and chopped

3 garlic cloves, minced

1 pound dried red kidney beans, soaked overnight in cold water

10 cups water

1 ham bone end, ham hock, or cured pork product of some kind (2 to 3 slices of bacon will work, too)

2 teaspoons Tabasco sauce, plus more for serving

2 teaspoons coarse salt

1 teaspoon dried thyme

1 bay leaf, crushed

1 recipe Basic White Rice (see page 187)

Halved, grilled seared sausage (optional)

Hot sauce, for serving

1 Heat a large pot. Swirl in the oil. Add the onion, celery, bell pepper, and garlic and sauté until soft and lightly caramelized, 11 to 12 minutes.

2 Drain and discard the soaking liquid from the beans and add the beans to the pot. Pour in the fresh water and stir. Bring to a boil, reduce the heat, and simmer uncovered for 1 hour. Skim off any foam as it rises to the surface.

3 Add the ham bone, Tabasco sauce, salt, thyme, and bay leaf. Continue to cook until the beans are soft and tender, 30 to 60 minutes more. (The time will vary depending on the age of the beans, so taste frequently.) Using the back of a spoon or spatula, crush some of the beans against the side of the pan to create a slightly creamy consistency. *

Quick Soak Rinse the beans. Place in a large pot and cover in double the water. Bring to a boil, uncovered. Remove from the heat, cover, and let the beans soak for one hour. Proceed with recipe.

rice and noodle pilaf

makes 2 quarts

This is one of my husband's fall-back, always-works-for-him recipes. It rounds out any meal and makes a perfect breakfast with a fried egg on top. He learned it from his Armenian friend Rich from Fresno, California. Its secrets: Put in a lot of butter. Cook the onions and broken noodles longer than you might think necessary, until that nutty smell comes off them. Stir constantly. Keep the heat high. Build the flavor before adding the rice and liquid.

3 tablespoons unsalted butter

½ yellow onion, chopped (about ¾ cup)

1 cup dried vermicelli noodles, broken into roughly 1-inch pieces

2 cups long-grain white rice

3 cups chicken broth

1 teaspoon coarse salt

1 Heat a large skillet over medium-high heat, add 2 tablespoons of the butter, and as soon as the butter melts, add the onion. Cook, stirring constantly, until the onion is translucent, 2 to 3 minutes. Add the noodles, lower the heat to medium, and cook, stirring constantly, until the noodles are golden brown and the mixture gives off a nutty aroma, 5 to 8 minutes.

2 Add the rice, stir to combine, and add the remaining tablespoon of butter.

3 Stir in the chicken broth and salt. Raise the heat to high and bring to a full rolling boil. Cover, reduce the heat to low, and simmer for 20 minutes, or until the rice and vermicelli have absorbed all the liquid. Fluff with a fork and serve. *

YOUR SPECIALTY

Even if you don't plan to cook on a regular basis, choose one recipe that you love and perfect it. You'll become famous for that one thing and you'll have something to "pull out of your back pocket" when you need it. Maybe you can only make a kick-ass pan-fried steak, as on page 146? To please most guys, pancakes could be your only specialty, but you'll be remembered for your weekend breakfasts. All you need is one dish, be it tuna melt, chicken soup, spaghetti and meatballs, an omelet, or apple pie.

fat girl red rice

serves 6 to 8

One night when we were having plain roast chicken and some sautéed kale for dinner, I wanted to make the rice a little more interesting. I added ingredients that I had on hand to enhance a recipe for Basic White Rice (page 187). The sun-dried tomatoes reddened the rice. The outcome combined so well with the Fried Kale (page 211) that I couldn't stop eating it. Hence the "fat girl" in its name.

1 tablespoon extra-virgin olive oil

¼ onion, chopped (about ⅓ cup)

1 garlic clove, minced

2 cups long-grain white rice

4 oil-packed sun-dried tomato halves, finely chopped

2 tablespoons tomato paste

1 teaspoon coarse salt

3 cups chicken broth

1 Heat a medium pot over medium-high heat and add the olive oil. When the oil is hot, add the onion and garlic. Cook and stir until translucent, 3 to 4 minutes. Add the rice and stir to toast it and coat it with the oil, about 90 seconds.

2 Stir in the sun-dried tomatoes, tomato paste, and salt. Stir and cook to fully incorporate, about 1 minute.

3 Add the chicken broth. Raise the heat to high, bring to a boil, and lower the heat to allow the rice to briskly simmer until holes form on top of it, about 5 minutes. Reduce the heat to very low, cover, and cook for about 15 minutes, or until all the liquid is absorbed. Fluff with a fork and serve. ∗

Sun-Dried Tomatoes A favorite pantry item, sun-dried tomatoes (which, along with balsamic vinegar, rank as an often-abused ingredient) have a deep roasted earthy flavor and can be purchased in different forms and degrees of quality.
- Packed in oil
- Packed dry; must be plumped for 10 minutes in boiled water, then drained
- Puréed

To make your own oven-dried tomatoes, preheat the oven to 300°F. Wash and dry 3 pounds of Roma tomatoes. Halve the tomatoes lengthwise and drain, cut sides down, on wire racks set over rimmed baking sheets for 15 minutes. Place the tomato halves on the baking sheets in a single layer and roast, turning once, for about 2 hours, until the tomatoes have given up most of their moisture. Let cool, cover in olive oil, then store in an airtight plastic container. Use refrigerated tomatoes within 1 month, or freeze dried tomatoes without oil for up to 3 months. To rehydrate dried tomatoes, cover with boiling water for 15 minutes. Drain and cover with olive oil.

Don't Hide
the Vegetables

Don't hide the vegetables; bring them forward in all their delicious glory. Change a name if you have to. Our middle son hated onions as a five-year-old, but he loved Brooklyn. So we told him that *these* onions come from Brooklyn, so he loved "Brooklyn onions."

When your kids are young, keep many varieties of colorful crunchy and crispy vegetables available for snacks instead of sugary, salty choices. Sliced cucumber, red bell peppers, and celery can fill up a boy and boost his energy until dinner without ruining his appetite. This should be the first response to the common cry, "I'm starving." Just cut a load of raw vegetables into different shapes and pile them into a bowl. Even if what follows is Cheetos (they always find it somewhere) or some other processed snack, at least you got the vegetables in.

A dinner plan should include one, preferably two, vegetables. When I returned to working full time, our youngest son was seven years old and my husband started cooking many of the family dinners. In the beginning, he'd say in frustration, "But they won't eat the vegetables. I'm sick of cooking them when no one will eat them." Put them on the table, night after night, is what I said—and never stop. That is what he did, and eventually we were successful: one of the first things our boys ask for when they return home from college or a long trip is fresh cooked vegetables.

BETTER BROCCOLI ABUNDANCE

- Buy a whole fresh head of broccoli, not precut and packaged or frozen.
- Trim the bottom of the stem. Holding the stem in your hand, the florets pointed away from you, with a sharp knife, shave off the florets into bite-sized pieces. With a knife or potato peeler, remove the tough skin from the stem and thinly slice the stem into ¼-inch-thick coins.
- In a saucepan, boil ½ inch of water. Line the bottom with the coins, top with the florets, and cover. Steam until just tender, not crunchy but not overcooked. (When you can smell the broccoli, it is generally done.)
- Drain off the cooking liquid, transfer the broccoli to a bowl, and toss with olive oil.

italian fries

serves 6 (if you are very lucky)

My oldest brother, Jim, is proof positive that if you cook well for a boy, he'll want to cook for himself. Presently this six-foot-five father of three strapping teenage boys effortlessly turns out delicious meals day in and day out for his own family. His sons are athletes who eat a ton—but their meals are always fresh and prepared with love. When our extended families gather to prepare a meal, their father is always at the forefront, planning and executing. My parents taught all three of my brothers to cook and eat well, but Jim has perfected my mom's specialty—a twist on oven fries originated by our Italian relatives. Everyone goes crazy for them, and there are never enough!

6 or 7 Idaho potatoes, peeled and sliced into ⅓-inch-thick French fry–style strips (see Potato Prep), soaked in cold salted water

4 tablespoons (¼ cup) extra-virgin olive oil

1 tablespoon dried Italian herbs or some combo of dried oregano, thyme, marjoram, and basil

2 cups freshly grated Romano cheese

¼ cup fresh parsley leaves, finely chopped

4 tablespoons (½ stick) salted butter, cut into 6 cubes

Coarse salt and freshly ground black pepper

1 Preheat the oven to 400°F.

2 Drain the potatoes and pat dry with paper towels. Spread 1 tablespoon of the olive oil on each of 2 rimmed baking sheets and spread out the potatoes. Overlapping is fine.

3 Sprinkle the dried herbs evenly over the potatoes. Liberally spread the cheese and parsley on top. Drizzle the remaining 2 tablespoons of olive oil over the cheese. Scatter the cubed butter around the pans.

4 Bake until the potatoes are golden brown, rotating the pans after 30 minutes, for 45 to 50 minutes total. Use a spatula to lift off the potatoes with all the crusty cheese adhered to them. Sprinkle with salt and pepper to taste. Serve hot. ∗

Potato Prep For a French-fry cut, peel the potatoes and slice lengthwise into ⅓-inch-thick slices. Stack the slices on top of one another, a few at a time, and slice lengthwise into ⅓-inch-thick strips. Peeled and sliced potatoes can turn brown pretty quickly. To avoid this, try floating the peeled, cut pieces in cold, salted water. When you're ready to cook, drain them and pat dry.

chunky mashed potatoes

serves 5 to 8

These are the mashed potatoes we grew up on, a true testament to my partially WASP upbringing. My mom always put cottage cheese—not milk or sour cream or anything else—in our mashers. We also liked them chunky, not smooth. Until I was an adult, I thought it was the normal way to eat mashed potatoes, and only altered my habits when my husband began substituting ricotta cheese for cottage cheese. Give it a try before you snarl; it's a good heap of protein on top of the deliciousness.

5 4- to 5-inch russet or Idaho potatoes, washed well but not peeled

4 tablespoons (½ stick) unsalted butter, softened

⅓ cup milk

1 cup (8 ounces) small-curd cottage cheese or ricotta cheese

Coarse salt and freshly ground black pepper

1 Place the potatoes in a large pot and cover with water. Bring to a boil and cook until the potatoes are tender, about 45 minutes. Insert a knife into the center of the potatoes to ensure accurate soft tenderness; the potatoes should be soft but not falling apart. Drain. When cool enough to handle, hold each potato in a clean kitchen towel and peel off the skin. Cut into chunks. (If in a hurry, peel the potatoes first and cut into small chunks for boiling.)

2 Add the butter and milk to the same pot and place over the lowest heat to melt the butter and warm the milk. Return the potatoes to the pot and mash until almost smooth. Add the cottage cheese and stir to combine. Season with salt and pepper. Stir briskly before serving. *

Getting Protein into Kids A dollop of high-protein low-fat cottage cheese or ricotta is a smart way to get protein into kids. With a gentle, friendly flavor, the half cup used to top a large baked potato contains a whopping 16 grams of protein, which makes it a wise alternative to meat and beans.

smashed potatoes

serves 6

This is a clever and simple preparation with multiple uses. Aside from being an excellent side dish on its own, it's really good under a fried egg and—don't laugh—as the basis for a small sandwich. The trick is to boil the potatoes enough to smash but not so much that they fall apart when they're sautéed.

1½ pounds small Yukon Gold potatoes

2 tablespoons unsalted butter

1 tablespoon extra-virgin olive oil

4 garlic cloves

Coarse salt and freshly ground black pepper

1 Put the whole potatoes in a medium pot, cover with water, and place over high heat. Bring to a boil and cook until the potatoes are just tender, 15 to 20 minutes.

2 Drain the potatoes. When they are cool enough to handle, place them on a cutting board and lightly smash with the side of a sturdy knife to flatten slightly.

3 Heat a large saucepan, and then add the butter and olive oil. Add the potatoes and whole garlic cloves. Season with salt and pepper. Cook until the potatoes are golden, about 4 minutes per side. Keep stirring the garlic around the pan to flavor the potatoes but do not allow it to burn. Discard the garlic and serve the potatoes immediately. *

cheesy scalloped potatoes

serves 6

This baked potato dish, another staple from my childhood, was a classic partner with glazed ham. It can be assembled in advance, covered, and held in the refrigerator overnight. Just make sure the potatoes are weighted down with a heavy dish to submerge in the milk and prevent discoloration. Bake before dinner, but leave enough time for the mixture to rest after cooking. You can layer in other cooked vegetables or diced meats, such as sautéed leeks or cooked bacon.

5 tablespoons unsalted butter

1 medium onion, peeled and sliced

1 cup cream

1 cup milk

5 medium Yukon Gold potatoes, peeled and thinly sliced (2½ to 3 pounds)

Coarse salt and freshly ground black pepper

⅛ teaspoon ground nutmeg

½ pound high-quality melting cheese, such as Comté or Gruyère, grated (2½ cups)

1 Heat a medium skillet over low heat, and then add 4 tablespoons of the butter. Add the onion and sauté, still over low heat, until it is completely softened to translucent, but not browned, 10 to 15 minutes. Set aside to cool.

2 Preheat the oven to 375°F. Butter an oval 12-cup baking dish.

3 In a large measuring cup with a spout, combine the cream and milk. Coat the bottom of the dish with a little of the cream mixture. Cover the bottom of the dish with one third of the potatoes, slightly overlapping each slice. Sprinkle on salt and pepper and half of the nutmeg. Layer over half of the onions and one third of the cheese and the cream mixture. Repeat. Top with the remaining potatoes and with the remaining cheese and cream mixture. Season with salt and pepper.

4 Dot with pieces of the remaining butter. Cover with foil and bake for 30 minutes. Remove the foil and bake for another 30 minutes, or until the top is brown, the cream is bubbling, and the potatoes are tender when tested with a thin knife. Let rest for at least 15 minutes before serving. ∗

grilled portobello mushroom steaks

serves 6 to 8 as a side dish

For the vegetarian invited to your meat barbecue, this is a great and satisfying "steak" alternative. It also makes an excellent side dish for any dinner. The dish can also be baked in the oven for 30 minutes at 400°F.

4 tablespoons extra-virgin olive oil

3 tablespoons fresh lemon juice

1 teaspoon coarse salt

½ teaspoon freshly ground black pepper

10 portobello mushrooms, stems removed, wiped free of dirt

6 to 8 sprigs of fresh herb such as sage or oregano

1 lemon, cut into wedges

1 In a baking dish large enough to hold the mushrooms in a single layer, whisk together the olive oil, lemon juice, salt, and pepper. Lay in the mushrooms, top down, and scatter half the fresh herbs on top. Marinate for about 20 minutes.

2 Prepare an outdoor grill or indoor grill pan. Remove the mushrooms from the marinade. Grill the mushrooms for 20 to 25 minutes, turning once. Remove from the grill to a platter. Squeeze fresh lemon juice over the mushrooms and scatter on the rest of the fresh herbs. Serve hot or at room temperature. *

spiced sweet potato wedges

serves 6 to 8

A fantastic accompaniment to grilled pork or roast chicken, these salty-sweet wedges also make a stealthily healthy snack for ravenous boys. The sweet potato truly is a super vegetable: it is packed with antioxidants and four times the daily recommendation of beta-carotene needed for healthy skin, hair, and eyesight. In several vegetable rating roundups, it consistently beat most other vegetables in overall nutritional power. No wonder it's one of the first foods we feed to babies.

2 tablespoons brown sugar

1 teaspoon coarse salt

½ teaspoon ground cumin

⅛ teaspoon cayenne pepper

4 medium sweet potatoes, peeled, sliced in half lengthwise, and cut into wedges about 4 inches long

1 tablespoon vegetable oil

1 Preheat the oven to 350°F. Cover a rimmed baking sheet with baking parchment or foil.

2 In a large bowl, combine the brown sugar, salt, cumin, and cayenne. Spread the sweet potatoes on the baking sheet. Drizzle the oil over the wedges and toss to coat.

3 Transfer the wedges to the bowl and toss completely with the spice mixture to coat each piece. Return the potatoes to the baking sheet and spread out in a single layer.

4 Bake for 10 minutes. Turn over the wedges. Raise the heat to 400°F. Bake for 10 to 15 more minutes, until the potatoes are golden brown and tender. ★

OTHER WAYS WITH SWEET POTATOES

● Bake whole in the oven: Wash the sweet potato, dry it, then poke it in a few places with a fork so it doesn't explode. (Yes, they do explode. Trust me.) Bake at 375°F for 50 to 60 minutes, until the potato is tender when pricked with a thin knife and its seepage is caramelized. It should be really soft on the inside and gooey under the skin. Then drizzle with soy sauce.
● Bake whole, slice open, and fill with steamed broccoli. Melt your favorite cheese over the top.
● Peel, cube, boil, mash, and use in place of mashed pumpkin for pie, flan, or cheesecake.

caramelized cauliflower
plain and fancy
serves 4 to 6

PLAIN

The cauliflower part one of this recipe is a revelation to all who believe they hate the vegetable. When we first made this dish for our kids, it became an instant hit. It's hard to resist its salty, sweet, crusted golden flavor.

1 head of cauliflower, washed, trimmed, cored, and thinly sliced (pieces will crumble; doesn't matter)

1½ tablespoons extra-virgin olive oil

Coarse salt and freshly ground black pepper

Preheat the oven to 400°F. Spread the cauliflower in an even layer on a rimmed baking sheet. Drizzle over the olive oil and sprinkle with salt and pepper. Toss to combine. Roast until the cauliflower is lightly caramelized, turning once, about 30 minutes. Serve as is or proceed with the variation below. *

FANCY

One summer night, looking for a change, I added some Sicilian flavors to the basic cooked vegetable. We served it at room temperature and loved it.

You can also substitute escarole greens for the chopped, sauteed cauliflower; then stir and cook until tender, about 12 minutes. Add to the hot pot with capers and raisins.

1½ tablespoons extra-virgin olive oil

1 garlic clove, minced

¼ teaspoon crushed red pepper flakes

2 tablespoons salt-packed capers, well rinsed

3 tablespoons golden raisins

1 recipe Carmelized Cauliflower Plain

1 tablespoon chopped fresh parsley leaves

1 Heat a small pan, and then add the olive oil, garlic, and red pepper flakes. Sauté for 30 seconds. Add the capers and raisins and cook for another minute.

2 Drizzle the caramelized cauliflower with the caper mixture and parsley and toss to coat well. Serve warm or at room temperature. *

Plain Carmelized Cauliflower (this page) and Ginger Garlic Glazed Green Beans (page 214)

oven-roasted vegetables

serves 5 and then some

Oven-roasting vegetables is a simple technique that makes efficient use of cooking space—the vegetables can share the oven with a chicken or pork roast—and results in deep flavor. Many vegetables can be oven-roasted; the keys are to cook at a high oven temperature and to be generous with the olive oil, salt, and pepper. I use different aromatics, such as shallots, garlic, or herbs, depending on what I have in the kitchen or what flavors work best with each vegetable. If you're cooking different types of vegetables, make sure the sizes and textures are similar so they're all done at the same time.

1 bunch of small carrots, peeled

4 medium beets, cleaned, trimmed, and quartered

8 ounces cremini mushrooms, trimmed, wiped clean, large ones halved

5 shallots, peeled and halved

¼ cup extra-virgin olive oil

1 tablespoon coarse salt

Coarsely ground black pepper

1 Preheat the oven to 400°F. Place each type of vegetable in its own area on a rimmed baking sheet. Drizzle the olive oil over all the vegetables. Sprinkle with the salt and pepper.

2 Roast until the vegetables are tender and lightly caramelized, 25 to 30 minutes. Test each type of vegetable for doneness. Arrange on a serving platter. *

Other Vegetables to Oven-Roast

● Brussels sprouts—The best! Cut in half, lengthwise. ● Asparagus—Snap off the fibrous ends. ● Broccoli—It works, but I prefer it steamed. ● Any root vegetable—Clean, cube, and season well. ● Scallions—Trim both ends and roast whole. ● Onions—Peel and slice or quarter. ● Potatoes—Small new potatoes can be whole or halved. Cut large potatoes crosswise into ¼-inch slices.

char-baked tomato, zucchini, and eggplant

serves 6 to 8

Even boys who think they hate zucchini and eggplant will love this combination. The vegetables, sliced very thin, stacked, and doused in olive oil, are roasted in a hot oven until they collapse; their juices get concentrated, and the whole becomes an alluring vegetable dish, more attractive than kids might find vegetables to be on their own. Critical to the success of this dish is to bake it way longer than you expect and keep pushing down the mixture with a spatula to release the moisture. By the time it is done, the vegetables will be thoroughly caramelized, soft and luscious, and the dish will be easy to cut into wedges or squares. This is superb as a side dish for fish and chicken or as the centerpiece of a vegetarian meal.

⅓ cup extra-virgin olive oil

1 onion, peeled and sliced

5 small tomatoes, thinly sliced

Coarse salt and freshly ground black pepper

1 small eggplant, about 6 inches long, thinly sliced crosswise

2 zucchini, about 5 inches long, thinly sliced lengthwise

2 garlic cloves, thinly sliced

½ teaspoon fresh thyme leaves

1 Preheat the oven to 400°F.

2 Pour some of the olive oil to cover the bottom of a 9 x 13-inch rectangular or 12-inch oval baking dish. Layer in half of the onion slices and one third of the tomatoes. Generously sprinkle with salt and pepper. Add a layer of eggplant and sprinkle on more salt. Add another third of the tomatoes, the zucchini, garlic, thyme, and the remaining onions. Top with the remaining tomatoes. Press down on the mixture with your hands. Pour over the remaining olive oil. Season generously with salt and pepper. (Don't worry. The vegetables will be piled high but collapse as they cook.)

3 Bake uncovered for 1½ hours. After 45 minutes, press the mixture down firmly with a spatula. The vegetables should be reduced in height, and should be brownish black and caramelized, almost charred in places. Return to the oven to finish roasting. Let cool for at least 10 minutes, so the mixture can solidify a bit. Cut into squares and serve. ✳

stuffed artichokes

serves 6

We serve these artichokes as the first course at our Easter meal, but they carry a deep flavor memory: I vividly recall my brothers and me, each at our own TV table, in an annual Christmas ritual watching *Rudolph the Red-Nosed Reindeer* and eating stuffed artichokes. Thanksgiving also featured this dish, deconstructed into a casserole (facing page).

1 lemon, halved

6 whole artichokes

¾ cup fresh bread crumbs

½ cup grated Pecorino Romano cheese

1 small garlic clove, minced

2 tablespoons chopped fresh parsley leaves

Freshly ground black pepper

1 Squeeze the lemon halves into a large bowl and fill the bowl with cold water. Trim the bottom off each artichoke. Trim off the tough outer leaves. Snip the thorny tips off the top leaves. As each one is completed, place it in the lemon water to prevent it from discoloring.

2 In a small bowl, combine the bread crumbs, cheese, garlic, and parsley and season with pepper. Pull each leaf open slightly from each artichoke and stuff a little filling into the openings. Place the artichokes snugly side by side in a large pan with a tight-fitting lid. Add 1 inch of water to the pot. Cover, bring to a boil, then reduce the heat and steam until the bottoms of the artichokes are tender, 35 to 45 minutes; a knife should insert easily. Make sure the water doesn't boil dry. Add more water if necessary.

3 Serve each artichoke hot, on an individual plate. ∗

ITALIAN GRATING CHEESE

- Parmesan cheese, made from cow's milk, is subtle and rich. It's available grated and in wedges. The flavor will be more pungent if the cheese is purchased in a wedge and grated as needed. I think it's best slivered and eaten on its own or with a slice of pear.
- Aged Romano cheeses, made from sheep's, goat's, and cow's milk (or a combination), also makes an excellent grating cheese, especially when you're looking for a more intense, salty, strong flavor. Romano cheese works beautifully in the artichoke stuffing (see page 208) or on Italian Fries (page 194) or in meatballs (see page 150). Often I use a combination of both cheeses to extract the best that both have to offer and I'll also substitute one for the other if needed.

MAKING HOMEMADE BREAD CRUMBS

There is no reason to pay for premade, store-bought bread crumbs, which usually lack flavor and texture. Whether you use fresh loaves or packaged sliced bread at home daily, accumulate the ends in a bag and freeze. When you have collected enough and have some extra time, break it into pieces using a knife or your bare hands and place into a food processor or blender jar. Pulse to the desired crumb size; generally I shoot for a resemblance to grains of rice. The results are better if done in small batches. To make by hand, place dry bread in a sealed bag. Smash with a rolling pin to break into crumbs. Place in a resealable bag, and store in the refrigerator for up to 1 month. If using fresh bread, place slices on a baking sheet and dry out slightly in a 300°F oven for 15 minutes. Cool and prepare as directed. You can store these in the freezer for up to 3 months.

ARTICHOKE CASSEROLE

Replace the fresh artichokes with three 9-ounce packages of frozen artichokes, thawed and drained. Double the amounts of bread crumbs, parsley, and cheese, and combine. Add 1 tablespoon fresh herbs or dried Italian herbs. Juice 2 lemons and whisk the juice with ⅔ cup olive oil and 2 minced garlic cloves. Layer the artichokes in one large (or two small) baking dishes. Toss together the bread-crumb mixture with the artichokes. Pour the dressing over all. Bake at 325°F, covered, for 30 minutes. Raise the heat to 375°F, uncover the dish, and cook for 20 minutes more, or until the bread crumbs are golden brown.

tomato onion stew

serves 6 (makes 1 quart)

This relish-like condiment makes a wonderful accompaniment to Miss Lamie's Fried Chicken (page 117) or a plain roast or grilled meat, adding color along with a tangy, acidic flavor.

3 tablespoons vegetable oil

3 medium onions, thinly sliced

1 garlic clove, minced

5 medium tomatoes, cut lengthwise into eighths

1½ teaspoons coarse salt

½ teaspoon freshly ground black pepper

1 Heat a large skillet over medium-high heat. Add the oil and swirl to coat the pan. Add the onions and sauté until translucent and soft, 3 to 5 minutes. Add the garlic and stir for another minute.

2 Add the tomatoes and cook until soft and the juice is slightly evaporated, 5 to 7 minutes. Stir in the salt and pepper. You can serve the mixture hot or cold. It will keep in the refrigerator for about 1 week. *

fried kale

serves 6 to 8

Kale has an earthy flavor and hearty texture. So many wonderful varieties of kale are available in the market these days. I love them all, but I especially love the dinosaur or Tuscan kale, which is dark green with long thin leaves. Cooking this vegetable well seems so simple, but it requires care and attention to bring it just to the right point. Many people first blanch it in boiling water to tenderize and soften the flavor before sautéing. Generally, I think this is a waste of time, and it also eliminates many of kale's valuable nutrients.

1 tablespoon extra-virgin olive oil

2 garlic cloves, thinly sliced

2 bunches of kale, average size, ends trimmed, sliced into 1-inch pieces

½ teaspoon coarse salt

Heat a large skillet over medium heat. Add the olive oil and garlic and stir constantly for 30 seconds. Little by little add the kale, increasing the heat to high. The kale will collapse as it hits the heat. Stir in the salt. When all the kale is in the pan, cover and cook, stirring occasionally, for 10 minutes, or until the leaves are tender but still dark green and slightly firm. Serve hot. ∗

Kale Chips For surprising crispy kale, clean slices of Tuscan kale as directed above, then toss in olive oil plus salt and pepper. Spread out over 2 baking sheets. Roast in a 400°F oven for 15 minutes until tender and crisp.

braised collard greens

serves 6

These are good with or without the bacon, though who could argue with the flavor of pork. I use bacon for convenience, but a ham hock would be the authentic choice here. This same basic recipe can be used for mustard greens, Swiss chard, dandelion greens, and beet greens. Adjust the cooking time down by a few minutes to achieve the tenderness you desire.

1 pound collard greens, trimmed and washed, water still clinging to the leaves

1 tablespoon vegetable oil

1 medium onion, chopped

3 slices bacon, cut in half lengthwise and sliced crosswise in ½-inch pieces

Pinch of crushed red pepper flakes

1 tablespoon red wine vinegar

Coarse salt

1. Remove the tough stems from the collard leaves. Finely slice the stems crosswise. Stack a few leaves on top of each other and cut into 1½- to 2-inch pieces. Repeat with all leaves. You'll have 8 packed cups.

2. Heat a 10-inch sauté pan over high heat. Swirl in the oil and add the onion, bacon, and red pepper flakes. Fry until the onion is soft and the bacon is beginning to render its fat and crisp up, about 13 minutes.

3. Add the greens, 2 cups at a time. Stir into the onion mixture as you add. They will collapse and shrink in the heat.

4. When all the greens are in the pan and the heat has returned to sizzling high, pour in the vinegar. Stir to evaporate. Cover and let the greens cook over low heat until just tender, 10 to 15 minutes. Add a bit of water as needed to keep the greens from burning. Add salt to taste and serve. *

Vegetarian Version If I omit the bacon, I use diced red bell pepper and/or diced tomato to make a seasoning base. Mince ½ red bell pepper or 1 tomato, or a combination of the two, and add to the pan in place of the bacon in Step 2. Cook for 8 instead of 13 minutes before proceeding to Step 3.

creamed spinach

serves 6

This tender spinach, suspended in a light, silky, creamy cloud, is reminiscent of Stouffer's popular frozen creamed spinach. Clean and steam the spinach in advance, make the béchamel (white sauce), fold it all together at the last minute, and heat it through. Serve with potatoes and any plain cooked meat. Anyone who frequents New York City steakhouses knows that creamed spinach and hash browns complete steak for the quintessential steakhouse meal.

2½ pounds fresh spinach, washed, water still clinging to the leaves

FOR BÉCHAMEL

3 tablespoons unsalted butter

¼ cup all-purpose flour

1 cup milk

1 teaspoon coarse salt

Pinch of freshly ground black pepper

Pinch of ground nutmeg

1 Steam the spinach in a large pot for 2 to 4 minutes, until the leaves have all collapsed. The water clinging to the leaves will be enough to cook it. Drain, cool, and squeeze out the liquid in a strainer. Coarsely chop the spinach.

2 To make the béchamel, heat a sauté pan over medium heat, and then melt the butter and whisk in the flour. Cook, stirring, for 1 minute. Whisk in the milk until fully incorporated and simmer for 30 seconds. Stir in the salt, pepper, and nutmeg.

3 Fold in the spinach and serve immediately. ∗

Spinach Spinach could be the most poorly handled vegetable in an inexperienced cook's repertoire. Nothing is worse than serving it soft and sandy. But fresh spinach, properly cleaned, lightly steamed just to collapse and tenderize it, drizzled with olive oil and maybe a squeeze of lemon juice, is truly delicious. A lot of fresh spinach cooks down to a little, so make enough—at least a couple of pounds.

- To wash properly, fill a large bowl with cold water, add the spinach, toss it around, and let it rest for a few minutes. Lift the spinach out to a colander, leaving the dirt behind. Repeat two or three times, if necessary, until the water is clear.
- When you return from grocery shopping, wash the leaves. To store, layer on a clean kitchen towel, roll the towel, and place in a plastic bag in the fridge.
- To steam, leave water clinging to the leaves. Place in a large pot over high heat and cover. Don't walk away—the greens get tender and toothsome when just collapsed from the steam really fast, 3 to 4 minutes. Oversteaming separates the moisture from the leaves and results in the gloppy, mushy mess that makes boys think they hate spinach.
- To prepare cooked spinach in advance for another recipe, press the spinach free of moisture, place in a covered container, and refrigerate.

ginger garlic glazed green beans

serves 4 to 6

One of my sons called looking for a green bean recipe that could accompany the Vietnamese lemongrass chicken that he was making from a cookbook. I rattled off a few ideas, and this recipe for Ginger Garlic Glazed Green Beans is what he created.

2 teaspoons peanut or vegetable oil

½ inch of fresh ginger, peeled and grated

3 garlic cloves, half sliced and half minced

1 pound green beans, rinsed and stemmed, with water still clinging to them

1 tablespoon soy sauce

¼ teaspoon toasted sesame oil

1 Heat a large sauté pan over medium heat. Add the oil, ginger, and minced garlic and sauté for 30 seconds. Raise the heat to medium-high, add the beans and sliced garlic, and stir-fry for 2 minutes.

2 Add ¼ cup water to the pan. Cook for another 4 minutes, partially covered. With 1 minute left, add the soy sauce and sesame oil and swirl around the pan to form a glazy sauce. *

Fresh Ginger and Garlic

Both flavorings will keep a long time if stored correctly, ginger in the refrigerator and garlic in a cool, dry place. Stock these simple ingredients, and you'll be able to make lots of Asian-flavored recipes.

Blanching

The blanching technique entails briefly cooking a fresh vegetable in boiling water to remove its raw texture while retaining the color and nutrients. Cover and let boil for about a minute. Then submerge the vegetable in ice water to stop the cooking and drain.

new orleans—style string beans

serves 4 to 6

Our youngest son's soccer coach had coached him for several seasons before I discovered the man's passion for cooking. When I asked what his favorite recipes were, he automatically mentioned this one. It's absolutely sensational. He wrote out the recipe for me; it describes the beans as having a "spicy-sweet taste and good texture. They cool off quickly and are best eaten when cooled off, so no need to rush to serve them hot."

1½ pounds green beans, stem ends removed

8 garlic cloves

4½ teaspoons extra-virgin olive oil (enough to lightly cover the pan)

3 tablespoons honey

2 teaspoons Tony Chachere's Creole Seasoning (see Note)

¼ cup cognac

NOTE: Tony Chachere's Creole Seasoning is available in most well-stocked supermarkets. To make an equivalent spice mixture, combine ½ teaspoon coarse salt, ¼ teaspoon freshly ground black pepper, ¼ teaspoon freshly ground white pepper, a pinch of cayenne pepper, and a large pinch of paprika.

1 Bring a large pot of salted water to a boil. Add the beans and garlic. Blanch for 3 minutes and drain.

2 Heat a large sauté pan over medium heat. Add the olive oil, honey, and the spice mixture. Let the honey "melt" together with the olive oil and spices.

3 Pat the drained beans and garlic cloves dry with paper towels, add them to the pan, and toss gently to coat them in the honey-spice mixture, 3 to 4 minutes.

4 Turn off the burner, pour the cognac into the pan, and flambé the beans until the alcohol is burned off. To flambé, ignite the alcohol by carefully touching the edge of the pan with the flame of a match or lighter. Novices are best off using fireplace matches or wooden kitchen matches instead of flimsy paper ones. Place the beans and garlic in a dish and serve, drizzling the remainder of the honey-spice mixture over them. Season with extra salt, if needed. *

TRIMMING STRING BEANS

Only the tough stem end of a string bean needs to be removed before cooking.
The bottom tip is just a very narrow part of the bean.

shredded sautéed cabbage

serves 6 to 8

If you're sure you dislike cabbage, try this quick sauté. The vegetable retains some texture and has none of that sulfury taste and mushy texture of cabbage that's been improperly cooked. This is also a great snack or breakfast served with a couple of fried eggs on top.

4½ teaspoons vegetable oil

1 medium onion, sliced

1 tomato, chopped

1 inch of fresh ginger, peeled and minced (optional)

¼ teaspoon crushed red pepper flakes

1 small head of green cabbage, cored and thinly sliced (about 10 cups)

1½ teaspoons coarse salt, plus more for serving

1 Heat a 14-inch skillet over medium-high heat, and then add the oil and onion. Sauté to soften the onion slightly, about 2 minutes. Stir in the tomato, ginger, if using, and red pepper flakes. Cook for an additional 2 minutes.

2 Add the cabbage and 1½ teaspoons salt. Stir to combine. Cover; reduce the heat to medium low, and cook, stirring occasionally as the cabbage begins to collapse. Add a little water, 2 tablespoons at a time, as needed if the cabbage becomes too dry. (This depends on the moisture level of the cabbage. You don't want it too wet.) Cook for approximately 13 minutes, or until the cabbage is just tender. Salt to taste and serve. ∗

cheddar corn bread

serves 6 to 8

We like this served with chili or even ribs. The addition of whole corn kernels makes the texture a little more interesting, but you can leave them out with no problem. Ditto the pickled jalapeños; and you can even switch the cheese for a different one. If you don't have a 10-inch cast-iron skillet, use an 8-inch square baking pan and adjust the baking time.

1 cup all-purpose flour

1 cup stone-ground yellow cornmeal

1 tablespoon sugar

1½ teaspoons baking powder

1 teaspoon coarse salt

Pinch of cayenne pepper

1½ cups milk

2 large eggs, lightly beaten

1½ tablespoons unsalted butter, melted

1 cup grated cheddar cheese

½ cup corn kernels (frozen, fresh, or left over from a cooked cob)

2 tablespoons chopped pickled jalapeños (optional)

1 Preheat the oven to 425°F.

2 In a large bowl, whisk together the flour, cornmeal, sugar, baking powder, salt, and cayenne. Blend in the milk, eggs, and butter. Fold in the cheese, corn, and the jalapeños, if using.

3 Place in a well-seasoned 10-inch cast-iron skillet or a buttered 8-inch square baking pan and smooth over the top. Bake for 35 to 45 minutes, until the top is golden brown and a cake tester inserted in the center comes out clean. Do not overbake or the corn bread will be dry. Cut into wedges or squares and serve hot. *

down-home desserts

they'll take it any way they can get it

And while any sweet treat will suffice most days, there's nothing like the appreciation a guy has for a little ole slice of pie, a piece of cake, a bowl of pudding, or fresh-baked cookies … when there's time. The wafting scents of home baking cement themselves firmly in the mind of a young boy.

I baked sweets often before the household swelled to five hungry mostly male mouths. It's hard enough to get dinner on the table most nights, let alone dessert, so I keep some simple choices in the house and bake the more extravagant down-home desserts when I have some extra time. Guys love homemade dessert and are happy to get it when they can, whether it's once a week, on birthdays, or at holiday time.

Here are some easy options:

1. Ice cream any time. I like the basics—chocolate, vanilla, or strawberry. The boys prefer as many bizarre add-ins as possible

2. Boiled-down frozen berries over ice cream

3. Root beer floats. Place a couple scoops of vanilla ice cream in a large glass then fill with root beer

4. Fruit sorbet or ice cream and club soda floats

5. Toast smeared with chilled chocolate glaze (see page 233) or Nutella chocolate hazelnut spread

6. Dark chocolate bar separated into pieces and mixed with toasted almonds

7. Cold salted popcorn tossed with chocolate chips

8. Sliced apples dusted with cinnamon

9. Ricotta cheese drizzled with honey and cocoa powder

10. Sliced strawberries in orange juice

11. Dates, nuts, and clementines laid out on a serving platter

12. Hot chocolate

13. Pears and Parmesan slices

14. Sliced bananas sautéed in butter, brown sugar, and cinnamon

15. Softened puréed dates spread on ginger snap cookies

16. Applesauce or jam mixed with yogurt

17. Grilled peaches or plums drizzled with pure maple syrup

18. Broiled grapefruit halves, topped with brown sugar

19. Pineapple chunks topped with shredded coconut

20. Brightly colored and weirdly shaped breakfast cereal (the kinds you'd never serve for breakfast)

basic pie dough
makes 1 double-crusted 9- or 10-inch pie

I use my foolproof Cream Cheese Pastry (page 65) for both savory and sweet pies; this is the other recipe I use only for sweet ones. The milk adds a little more fat, which helps with the pliability and gives you a little more grace when rolling out. Try making this both by hand and in a food processor; if you master both methods, you'll be ready to make pie regardless of what equipment— or lack thereof—is on hand. If you find yourself without a rolling pin, try a clean, dry wine or soda bottle, well floured, instead. Keep ingredients cold and work fast.

I prefer unbleached all-purpose flour, such as King Arthur or Bob's Red Mill.

2 cups all-purpose flour

1 teaspoon coarse salt

1 cup (2 sticks) very cold unsalted butter, cut into pieces

½ cup very cold milk or water

1 In a large bowl or in the bowl of a food processor, combine the flour and salt. Add the butter and cut in or pulse until the mixture resembles a coarse meal. (To *cut in* means to mix cold fat such as butter with dry ingredients to form small pieces.) Pour in the milk. Combine just until the dough holds together in a ball.

2 Turn the dough onto a piece of plastic wrap and lift the sides toward the middle to press them together. Cut the dough in half. Form each piece into a disk and wrap in plastic. Refrigerate for at least 15 minutes. If the dough has been refrigerated in advance, remove 15 minutes before using. The dough can be made and refrigerated for up to 3 days in advance or frozen for up to 6 weeks. *

MAKING DOUGH BY HAND

Cut the butter into the flour with a fork, two knives, or a pastry cutter. Or, use your fingertips and work fast. Pour the milk over the fat/flour particles. Use your whole hand to gather everything together and form the dough. Handle as little as required to make a solid mass. The dough is right if a piece can be pinched together and hold its shape. Proceed to Step 2.

old-fashioned apple pie

makes 1 double-crusted 10-inch pie

This is my husband's absolute favorite pie. He even prefers it to birthday cake. To qualify as a great apple pie, the mixture of apples should create a combined sweet-tart flavor balance. I like to use half tart and half sweet, and the apples should retain some structure when cooked. This old-fashioned apple pie isn't overly spiced, as I like to taste the apples first and foremost. Cook your pie long enough for the filling to fully bake and thicken. Let it sit and settle before cutting. Served slightly warm with the best vanilla ice cream, it's heaven. Or serve it with a wedge of cheddar cheese, like we did when I was a kid.

Juice of 1 lemon (2 tablespoons)

8 apples, 4 tart, 4 sweet

1 recipe Basic Pie Dough (page 223)

¼ cup sugar, plus 2 teaspoons for sprinkling

⅓ cup all-purpose flour, plus more for rolling out the dough

½ teaspoon ground cinnamon

Pinch of ground cloves

½ teaspoon coarse salt

1 tablespoon cold unsalted butter, cut into small pieces

1 large egg yolk

1 tablespoon milk

1 Preheat the oven to 350°F. Position the racks in the center of the oven and in the lower third.

2 Squeeze the lemon juice into a large bowl. Peel, quarter, core, and thinly slice one apple at a time. Toss the slices in the lemon juice to prevent browning. Repeat with each apple.

3 On a well-floured surface, roll out one piece of dough to about 12 inches in diameter and lay it in the bottom of a standard 10-inch pie plate. (See page 225 for detailed rolling instructions). Trim the edges of the dough flush with the edge of the pie plate's rim.

4 Add the ¼ cup sugar, the flour, cinnamon, cloves, and salt to the apples and toss to coat. Pile the apples into the dough-lined pie plate. Dot with the butter.

Apples So many wonderful varieties are available at the farmers' market and even at the plain old grocery store. Here are some good baking choices:
● **Sweet:** Golden Delicious, Rome Beauty, McIntosh, Gala, Fuji ● **Tart:** Granny Smith, Cortland, Winesap, Pippin ● **Sweet and tart:** Empire, Braeburn, Honey Crisp, Jonagold, Northern Spy

5 Roll out the top crust to a diameter of 12 inches. Lay it over the apples. Trim the edge of the top crust so it hangs over the bottom crust by at least ¾ inch. Tuck the top crust under the bottom and roll it under all around. Pinch it together to close. Crimp the edges with fingers or press with a fork. Chill the pie for a few minutes.

6 In a small bowl, whisk together the egg yolk and milk. Cut a few slits in the crust top to allow steam to escape during baking.

Brush the egg mixture evenly over the whole crust, being careful not to block the slits. Sprinkle with the remaining 2 teaspoons of sugar.

7 Place a cookie sheet on the lower rack to catch any overflowing juices from the pie. Place the pie on the center rack and bake for 1 hour and 15 minutes, or until the crust is golden brown and there is a sign of bubbling juices. Cool on a wire cooling rack for at least 1 hour. Slice and serve. ⋆

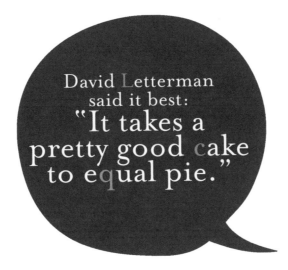

David Letterman said it best: "It takes a pretty good cake to equal pie."

HOW TO ROLL OUT DOUGH

Rub flour over a rolling pin. Place the dough disk on a clean, well-floured surface. Applying some pressure with the rolling pin, roll gently from the center of the dough to the top and bottom edges. Rotate the disk and roll to the top and bottom edges again. Turn the dough over, re-flour the surface and rolling pin, and continue to roll the dough from the center out to the edges. Turn over and roll again, rotating the disk to assure even rolling until the dough is about 12 inches in diameter and thin but not transparent. Roll dough up on rolling pin to transport to pie tin.

strawberry rhubarb pie

makes one 9-inch pie with a lattice top or with a double crust

I adore this pie, which I start making in June, when fresh strawberries come into season on the heels of May's rhubarb. Early on in life, I discovered that cooking special things made both other people and me happy—and the fact that you took the time to do it (instead of just stopping off at the bakery) shows you care. For years I made my dough by hand, a skill that is handy to master; but now I use a food processor if it's available. Serve the pie with a scoop of vanilla ice cream.

1 recipe Basic Pie Dough (page 223)

3 cups sliced strawberries

4 cups sliced rhubarb

1½ cups sugar, plus 2 teaspoons for sprinkling

½ cup all-purpose flour, plus more for rolling out the dough

1¼ teaspoons coarse salt

2 tablespoons unsalted butter, cut into small pieces

1 large egg yolk

1 tablespoon milk

1 Preheat the oven to 425°F. Position the racks in the center of the oven and in the lower third.

2 On a well-floured surface, roll out one piece of dough to about 11 inches in diameter and lay it in the bottom of a 9-inch pie plate. (See page 225 for detailed rolling instructions.) Trim the edges of the dough flush with the edge of the pie plate's rim. Roll out the other piece of dough. Cut it into strips for a lattice crust, if desired, or leave intact.

3 In a large bowl, combine the strawberries, rhubarb, and the 1½ cups sugar. Stir in the flour and salt, coating most of the fruit. Place the fruit in the dough-lined pie plate. Dot with the butter.

4 To make a lattice crust, lay half the strips of dough across in one direction, half in the other. Carefully weave them in and out of each other to create a basketweave pattern. Or, lay the entire piece of dough over the filling to create a top crust. Trim the edges of the top crust or dough strips so they hang over the bottom crust by at least ¾ inch. Tuck the top crust edges under the bottom crust and roll under all around. Pinch together to close. Crimp the edges with fingers or press with a fork. Chill the pie for a few minutes.

5 In a small bowl, whisk together the egg yolk and milk. If using an entire crust, cut slits in the top to allow steam to escape during baking. Brush the egg mixture evenly over the lattice or crust, being careful not to block the slits. Sprinkle with the remaining 2 teaspoons of sugar.

6 Place a cookie sheet on the lower rack to catch any overflowing juices from the pie. Place the pie on the center rack and bake for 20 minutes, then reduce the heat to 400°F. Continue to bake until golden brown and cooked through, 50 to 60 more minutes. Cool on a wire cooling rack for 1 hour before serving. ∗

Rhubarb Combo

Rhubarb alone is a pie that only purists covet. But rhubarb mixed with berries is a popular and flavorful combination of both tart and sweet. For this pie, raspberries, blueberries, blackberries, or cherries can be substituted for the strawberries.

Men Love Pie

My boys love desserts, and pie is their favorite hands down.

My husband says he longs for good pie. "There is so much bad pie out there," he frequently laments. He remembers his mother's apple pie and how great it was, with a very salty crust and perfect fruit. He also recalls her chocolate banana cream coconut pie, which consisted of delicious chocolate pudding with banana on it, topped with whipped cream and toasted coconut. Regular crust, not a graham cracker one.

Any great pie begins with a great crust, something that intimidates many a fine cook. The first pie dough I learned to make successfully was for a cream cheese crust (see page 65). I make it to this day and recommend it to anyone shy about trying crust. Its flavor is savory and crackerlike. But the real baking secret for many down-home crusts is lard: ask any old-school pie baker, and I'll bet his or her crust is made with it; I think the pies of my husband's childhood owe their success to it. Try substituting lard for some or all of the butter in a pastry recipe and see for yourself the difference it makes in flavor and texture.

Since I've worked alongside many skilled bakers, I've learned many other tricks of the trade:

- Work cold and fast. Keep all your ingredients cold, including the flour. Cold pieces of butter within the dough are what steams up in the baking and creates flakiness.
- Don't overmix the dough. Blend just until combined.
- Even if your dough doesn't fully combine into a ball, turn it out onto a large piece of plastic wrap. Gather the pieces and press it together.
- Wrap firmly in plastic wrap and chill for 30 minutes. If you made the dough in advance, remove it from the fridge 30 minutes before rolling. When pressed for time, I put freshly made dough in the freezer for 10 minutes before rolling.
- For fruit pies, make sure the ratio of thickener (cornstarch or flour) to fruit is correct. A general rule is 2 tablespoons cornstarch to 4 cups of berries or stone fruit or 1 cup flour to 3 pounds apples. Cornstarch thickens yet keeps the translucent jewel-colored juices of berries and stone fruits clear. It's so disappointing to cut into a pie in which the juice leaks out, separating from the fruit and making the crust soggy.
- After it comes out of the oven, let the pie sit out to cool long enough before cutting, to allow the juices to settle and the filling to slightly firm up.

banana cream pie

makes 1 9-inch single-crust pie

My nostalgia for cream pies comes from childhood dinners at the many classic roadhouses in our lakeside Canadian town. These pies are some of the easiest to master and are welcome any time of year. The crust is blind baked, which means it's lined and weighted down with dried beans or with pie weights and baked on its own without the filling. When the crust cools, a simple homemade pudding is spread in and topped with whipped cream.

½ recipe Basic Pie Dough (page 223)

¾ cup all-purpose flour, plus more for rolling out the dough

½ cup plus 1 tablespoon sugar

½ teaspoon coarse salt

2 cups milk

4 large egg yolks (reserve the whites for a meringue or other recipe)

2 tablespoons unsalted butter

1 teaspoon pure vanilla extract

2 ripe bananas

1 pint (2 cups) heavy cream

A Successful Cream Pudding Filling

To avoid producing a pie filled with either soup or wallpaper paste, the pudding filling must be cooked to just below the boiling point; at this point the mixture should coat the back of a wooden spoon. While it may seem too thin, it will thicken more as it cools.

1 Preheat the oven to 375°F. Position a rack in the center of the oven.

2 On a well-floured surface, roll out the dough to about 11 inches in diameter and lay it in the bottom of a 9-inch pie plate. (See page 225 for detailed rolling instructions.) Trim the edges of the dough to ½ inch over the edge of the pie plate's rim. Fold the dough under and gently pinch it together. Crimp the edges with your fingers or press with a fork all around. Prick the dough on the bottom twice with a fork.

3 Blind bake the crust: Line the dough in baking parchment or foil. Top with baking weights, dried beans, or rice to weight it down. Bake on the center rack for 20 minutes. Remove the weights and foil. Bake for 10 more minutes, or until the crust is golden. Cool on a wire cooling rack.

4 Meanwhile, whisk together the flour, the ½ cup sugar, and the salt in a medium saucepan. With the heat on low, slowly whisk the milk into the flour mixture and cook on low heat. Whisk in the egg yolks. Cook for 1 to 2 minutes, stirring constantly and incorporating the thickening mixture as it forms on the bottom and sides of the pan. The mixture should coat the back of a wooden spoon. Remove from the heat and stir in the butter and vanilla. Cool slightly.

5 Slice the bananas into the bottom of the pie crust. Pour the pudding over the bananas, smooth the top, and chill the pie.

6 Whip the cream with the remaining tablespoon sugar to form stiff peaks. Spread over the custard mixture. Chill completely and slice. *

apple crisp

serves 4 to 6

Satisfy his sweet tooth with a big, bubbling pan of a buttery, crisp-topped fruit dessert. If you're pie-shy, try this first. There's a lot of room for variation, and it doesn't require precision for success. Sliced fruit—pears or any type of stone fruit such as peach, plum, or nectarine work well—fills a buttered baking dish, and a quick topping is sprinkled on before it bakes. Oats and nuts in the topping make this a reasonably healthy dessert, too.

FRUIT

2 tablespoons fresh lemon juice

4 apples, 2 tart and 2 sweet (see page 224 for apple choices)

2 tablespoons granulated sugar

⅛ teaspoon ground cinnamon

¼ cup all-purpose flour

2 tablespoons cold unsalted butter, cut into small pieces

TOPPING

¾ cup rolled oats

½ cup brown sugar, light or dark

¼ cup walnuts or pecans, coarsely chopped

3 tablespoons all-purpose flour

½ teaspoon coarse salt

6 tablespoons cold unsalted butter, cut into small pieces

OPTIONAL TOPPING ADD-INS

¼ teaspoon ground cinnamon

⅛ teaspoon ground ginger

⅛ teaspoon freshly ground black pepper

Pinch of nutmeg

Pinch of ground cloves

1 Preheat the oven to 400°F. Position a rack in the center of the oven.

2 To prepare the fruit, place the lemon juice in a large bowl. Peel, core, and cut the apples into ½-inch wedges, tossing the pieces in the lemon juice as they are cut, to prevent browning.

3 To the apples, add the granulated sugar, cinnamon, and flour. Toss to combine and pour into a buttered 8 x 8-inch square or oval baking pan. Scatter the butter on top.

4 Make the topping in the same bowl. Combine the oats, brown sugar, nuts, flour, salt, and optional spices. Cut in the butter using a pastry blender, a fork, or two knives. Sprinkle the topping evenly over the fruit and bake on the center rack for 40 to 45 minutes, until the topping is dark golden and the apples are bubbling. Cool slightly on a wire cooling rack. Scoop out with a large spoon to serve in bowls. *

FRUIT AND TOPPING VARIATIONS
The rule of thumb is 3 parts fruit to 1 part topping to create a good texture. The topping is dry to absorb the juices. For a pear version, use 4 or 5 peeled Bosc pears. Switch lemon juice for lime, omit the cinnamon, and *double* the ginger in the topping. For peaches or nectarines, peel and slice 6 pieces of fruit, and toss in orange juice instead of lemon. Add 1 teaspoon of orange zest to the topping and increase the flour to ¼ cup. *

dolly's chocolate bundt cake

makes 1 large cake

I use this recipe (thanks to my first employer, Dolly) more often than any other for special birthdays and holiday baking. If you think you're just a competent or if you're a novice baker, this is the cake for you: it's easy to prepare, bakes in one pan, has a moist and tender texture, and requires only a glaze to finish. Its distinctive look is on the fancy side, which brings a little something extra to a birthday party or holiday table.

CAKE

1 cup (2 sticks) unsalted butter, softened

1½ cups sugar

4 large eggs

1 teaspoon pure vanilla extract

2½ cups all-purpose flour

½ cup unsweetened cocoa powder

½ teaspoon ground cinnamon

1 teaspoon baking soda

1 teaspoon coarse salt

½ cup chopped semisweet chocolate

½ cup chopped walnuts (optional)

1 cup buttermilk

GLAZE

1 cup finely chopped unsweetened chocolate

½ cup sugar

⅓ cup (5⅓ tablespoons) unsalted butter

⅔ cup heavy cream

2 tablespoons rum or brandy (optional)

Triple-Duty Glaze

This chocolate glaze also doubles as a spread or topping. Pour into a jar and refrigerate for up to 6 weeks. Spread on warm toast or reheat and drizzle on ice cream, layer into a sundae, or use as a dip for fresh strawberries.

1 Preheat the oven to 325°F. Butter a 12-cup Bundt pan.

2 To make the cake, in a large bowl, cream together the butter and sugar. Beat in the eggs, one at a time, and the vanilla. Scrape down the sides of the bowl.

3 In a separate bowl, whisk together the flour, cocoa, cinnamon, baking soda, and salt. Toss in the chopped chocolate and the walnuts, if using.

4 Into the butter mixture, alternately add the flour mixture and the buttermilk in three additions, ending with the flour. Mix just until everything is blended together; don't overmix.

5 Spoon the batter evenly into the Bundt pan and smooth the top of the batter. Bake for about 55 to 60 minutes, or until a cake tester or toothpick inserted into the cake comes out clean. Let the cake cool in the pan briefly. Turn out onto a cake plate to cool completely.

6 For the glaze, place a heat-proof bowl over a pot of simmering water. Add the glaze ingredients and stir to melt and combine. Drizzle over the top of the cooled cake and let the glaze set, 15 to 20 minutes, before serving. ★

busy-day chocolate cake

makes 1 8-inch square cake

This recipe dates back to the 1960s and features minimal cleanup—the ingredients get blended in the very pan that goes into the oven. It was the first cake I ever attempted to bake, and I frequently ate and enjoyed it as a child. I'd recommend it to novice bakers and to anyone pressed for time. I suggest using safflower oil, though the recipe specifically calls for Wesson oil. (Perhaps this originated in a Wesson oil cooking pamphlet.) Cool and frost with your favorite icing (my aunt Gina always used the buttercream recipe on the back of the box of confectioners' sugar). Also, this cake is vegan, too—no eggs, butter, or milk!

1½ cups all-purpose flour

1 cup sugar

3 tablespoons unsweetened cocoa powder

1 teaspoon baking soda

½ teaspoon coarse salt

6 tablespoons safflower oil or vegetable oil

1 teaspoon pure vanilla extract

1 tablespoon white vinegar

1 cup cold water

1 Preheat the oven to 350°F.

2 In an 8-inch square cake pan, whisk together the flour, sugar, cocoa, baking soda, and salt. Make a well in the center of the mixture.

3 Into the well, add the oil, vanilla, vinegar, and cold water. Whisk until well combined. Bake for 35 to 40 minutes, or until a cake tester or toothpick inserted in the center comes out clean. Cool completely in the pan on a wire rack before frosting. *

Best Chocolate Cake. Preheat oven 325°

1/2 tsp. salt
2 1/2 c. flour
1 tsp. Baking soda
1 1/2 cup cinnamon
1/2 t sugar

Chocolate
to chopped (opt.)
milk
Butter

Chocolate Pudding
3 1/2 Tbs. flour
3 Tbs. Cocoa
Salt (q.s.)
2 Tbs. butter
1 Egg (1)
1 1/2 cup milk
1 tsp. vanilla
sugar

Mix dry in
Add milk-
boiler till
butter stir
from fire-Ad
Egg-Cook few
1/2 cup choppe
be added if so

so makes a good filling for

tessy's banana bread
makes 1 loaf

When a boy smells banana bread baking, he'll hover until it comes out of the oven and he can get a slice. This is a simple go-to recipe for after-school snacks, bake sales, and school birthdays and for breakfast, too. It travels well, without falling apart, and it stays moist for several days. The topping gives it added flavor and crunch.

1 cup plus 1 tablespoon all-purpose flour

½ cup granulated sugar

¾ teaspoon baking powder

½ teaspoon baking soda

Coarse salt

4 tablespoons (½ stick) unsalted butter, melted, plus 1 tablespoon cold butter, cut into small pieces

⅓ cup buttermilk, mild, or a combination of plain yogurt and milk

1 large egg, lightly beaten

1 ripe banana, mashed (about ½ cup)

1 teaspoon pure vanilla extract

TOPPING

1 tablespoon brown sugar

¼ teaspoon ground cinnamon

Pinch of nutmeg

1. Preheat the oven to 300°F. Butter a 4½ x 8½-inch loaf pan.

2. In a large bowl, whisk together the 1 cup flour, the sugar, baking powder, baking soda, and ½ teaspoon salt.

3. Stir in the melted butter and the buttermilk. Add the egg and beat for 1 minute. Add the banana and vanilla. Stir until well combined. Spread the mixture evenly into the prepared pan.

4. Make a topping by mashing together the tablespoon of cold butter with the tablespoon of flour, the brown sugar, cinnamon, nutmeg, and a pinch of salt. Distribute the topping evenly over the batter. Bake for 40 to 45 minutes, or until a cake tester or toothpick stuck in the center comes out clean. Cool in the pan on a wire rack for 10 minutes. Cut and serve from the pan. *

Buttermilk If you can't find buttermilk in the store, or if you want to make your own alternative, mix 1 cup whole milk with 2 teaspoons lemon juice, white vinegar, or cream of tartar. Stir and let stand. Stir again and let stand for 15 more minutes before using.

Fresh leftover buttermilk makes a refreshing, healthful drink on its own. It's also good:
- To use instead of milk in pancake or waffle batter
- To tenderize and flavor poultry (see Quick Fried Chicken, page 116)
- To mix with a vegetable juice (such as tomato) for a quick cold soup topped with chopped scallion and dill

Bananas Old bananas have to be practically dissolving into the bowl *not* to be perfect for banana bread. Peel, mash, and freeze them if you don't have time to bake right away. If you have a surplus of just-ripe bananas, however, peel, chunk, and freeze them to use in smoothies.

peach shortcake

makes 8 individual shortcakes or one 8-inch-round shortcake

During that small window when peaches are at their peak of ripeness, very little needs to be done to them to create a spectacular summer dessert. My brothers and I remember the annual Essex County peaches from our grandfather's Ontario farm. Our grandmother peeled and sliced them, then doused them in Triple Sec to serve over ice cream. Now I slice them and spoon them over biscuits, topped with ice cream or whipped cream.

1 pound fresh ripe peaches, peeled and sliced

2 tablespoons fresh orange juice

2 tablespoons Triple Sec liqueur (optional)

1 recipe Flaky Buttery Biscuits (page 51), topped with cinnamon sugar before baking

1 tablespoon unsalted butter, softened

1 pint best-quality vanilla ice cream, slightly softened, or whipped cream

Fresh mint leaves, for garnish

1 Place the peaches in a bowl with the orange juice and the Triple Sec, if using. Let sit for a while, stirring occasionally.

2 If the biscuits aren't straight from the oven, heat them in the microwave for about 30 seconds. Slice open and butter the top side of each biscuit. Place each bottom on a plate. Place 2 small scoops of the ice cream onto each biscuit. Top with a large spoonful of peaches. Drizzle over some juice and top with the buttered top. If using whipped cream, place the peaches on the biscuit first. Serve immediately, garnished with mint. *

CHOOSING PEACHES

"If it doesn't smell like a peach, it won't taste like one" is a saying I think of when choosing all fruits and vegetables. But peaches may be the most fragrant of all; their sweet scent should permeate your nostrils regardless of how firm the fruit is. Buy them when they're only slightly firm to the touch; they ripen very quickly off the vine.

german apple cake

makes 1 8-inch-square cake

I bake this simple cake when the huge fruit bowl in the kitchen is emptying out more slowly than usual. It can also be made with plums or peaches.

1 cup all-purpose flour

1½ teaspoons baking powder

1 teaspoon coarse salt

8 tablespoons (1 stick) unsalted butter, softened

1⅓ cups sugar

2 large eggs, lightly beaten

1 teaspoon pure vanilla extract

1 teaspoon ground cinnamon

Juice of ½ lemon

3 to 4 tart apples, such as Granny Smith, Cortland, or Winesap

1 Preheat the oven to 375°F. Butter an 8-inch square pan or equivalent-size baking dish.

2 In a small bowl, whisk together the flour, baking powder, and salt. In a medium bowl, cream together the butter and 1 cup of the sugar. Stir in the eggs and vanilla. Add the flour mixture and beat until combined. Spread the mixture evenly in the prepared pan.

3 In a small bowl, combine the remaining ⅓ cup sugar with the cinnamon. Squeeze lemon juice into a medium bowl. Peel, core, and slice the apples into the bowl. Add the cinnamon-sugar mixture and toss to thoroughly coat each apple slice. Arrange the apple slices on top of the batter in overlapping rows, pressing lightly into the batter. Bake for about 45 minutes, until a cake tester or toothpick inserted in the center comes out clean. Cool in the pan on a wire rack for 10 to 15 minutes before serving. ∗

cream-puff pastry

makes 24 small puffs

It's pretty easy to learn to make this magical dough—not to mention that it lends itself to a clever do-ahead strategy: when you have some extra time, make the dough and form and freeze the puffs. The uncooked puffs go from the freezer to the oven and come out perfectly well, which makes the finished dish look effortless.

1 cup all-purpose flour

¼ teaspoon coarse salt

1 cup water

8 tablespoons (1 stick) unsalted butter, cut into small pieces

5 large eggs, at room temperature

The Many Uses of Cream Puffs

● **Éclairs:** 3- to 4-inch oblong shapes filled with pastry cream and topped with a sweet glaze (see following page) ● **Profiteroles:** round puffs filled with ice cream and topped with hot chocolate sauce ● **Gougères:** round bites made savory by folding shredded cheese into the batter; served as hors d'oeuvres ● **Cream puffs:** round puffs filled with sweetened whipped cream; slice the tops from the puffs and fill with the cream. Replace the tops and dust with confectioners' sugar.

1 Preheat the oven to 400°F. Prepare a pastry bag with a ½-inch tip (optional).

2 In a small bowl, whisk together the flour and salt. Place the water and butter in a medium saucepan and bring to a boil. Add the flour mixture and beat vigorously with a wooden spoon for several seconds, until the dough is smooth, pulls away from the sides of the pan, and begins to form a ball. Remove the pan from the heat. Cool the dough for a couple of minutes. Beat in the eggs one at a time, until smooth and glossy, 1 to 2 minutes.

3 Place the dough in the pastry bag. (Alternatively, you can use a spoon to form the puffs.) Grease 2 rimmed baking sheets or line with baking parchment. Pipe the desired shapes onto the baking sheets. The dough can be frozen at this point on the tray then collected into freezer bags and sealed.

4 For small (1½-inch) puffs, bake for 10 to 12 minutes. For a standard éclair shape, bake for 10 minutes, then raise the heat to 425°F and continue baking for 15 minutes total, or until puffed up, golden brown, and firm to the touch. Cool completely on a wire rack. ★

chocolate éclairs

makes 30 4-inch éclairs

Master a pastry-shop classic like this, and you've automatically upgraded your baking reputation. Each of the components—pastry, filling, and topping—can be made in advance and pulled together just before serving. Not exactly an everyday dessert, these chocolate indulgences should be trotted out for your family on special occasions, such as a significant anniversary, a graduation, or a Valentine's Day party.

30 4-inch oblong cream puffs (see page 241), baked and cooled

PASTRY CREAM

2 large whole eggs

8 large egg yolks (reserve the whites for another recipe)

⅔ cup sugar

½ cup all-purpose flour

3 cups milk, scalded

2 teaspoons pure vanilla extract

½ cup heavy cream

CHOCOLATE GLAZE

½ cup finely chopped unsweetened chocolate

¼ cup sugar

3 tablespoons unsalted butter

⅓ cup heavy cream

1. Using a serrated knife, slice the tops off each cream puff pastry and set both halves aside on baking sheets.

2. For the pastry cream, in a large bowl, lightly beat the eggs and egg yolks together. Add the sugar, a little at a time. Continue beating until the mixture falls in ribbons when the beater is lifted, about 5 minutes.

3. Mix in the flour. Add the milk in a steady stream.

4. Transfer the mixture to a large saucepan. Bring to a gentle boil over medium-low heat and cook, whisking constantly, until the mixture thickens, about 10 minutes.

5. Strain the pastry cream through a fine sieve into a large bowl. Stir in the vanilla. Press plastic wrap directly on the surface of the pastry cream to prevent it from forming a skin. Cool in the refrigerator for at least 1 hour.

6. In a medium bowl, whip the cream to form stiff peaks. Fold into the pastry cream (use a spatula to gently blend without deflating the whipped cream). Fill the bottom of each cream puff with the pastry cream.

7. For the glaze, place a heat-proof bowl over a pot of simmering water. Add the chocolate, sugar, butter, and cream and stir until melted and well combined. Dip the top of each éclair into the chocolate and place it over the cream-filled bottom. Place on a platter and chill until ready to serve. ✳

lemon soufflé pudding

serves 6

Soufflés can be difficult to bake properly, but this imposter is a snap to make. A lemon-lover's favorite, this light and delicate dessert may seem unmanly, but it makes a complementary finish to large mannish feasts, which are often rich and filling. The bottom is silky and pudding-like while the top has a light meringue-type soufflé thanks to a technique called *bain-marie* ("water bath") in which the baking dish is set inside a larger pan filled with hot water.

1 teaspoon unsalted butter, for the baking cups

5 large eggs, separated

¾ cup sugar

1 tablespoon freshly grated lemon zest

¼ cup fresh lemon juice

2 tablespoons confectioners' sugar, for dusting

Whipped cream, for garnishing

1 Preheat the oven to 350°F. Using the teaspoon of butter, butter six 2-ounce baking cups or one 12-ounce (8 x 10-inch) oval baking dish. Place the cups or dish in a roasting pan. Bring a tea kettle or medium pot of water to a boil.

2 Meanwhile, in a large bowl, beat the egg whites until stiff. In another clean bowl, beat the egg yolks until frothy and light in color, 3 to 4 minutes. Slowly add the sugar to the yolks while still beating. Mix in the lemon zest and juice.

3 Gently fold the egg whites into the egg yolk–lemon mixture. Pour the batter into each soufflé cup (filling each three-quarters full) or the baking dish. Put the roasting pan on the oven rack with the oven door open. Carefully and quickly pour the boiling water into the roasting pan to come halfway up the sides of the baking cups or dish. Slide the pan into the oven and bake for 20 to 25 minutes. Don't overcook.

4 Remove the pan from the oven. Set the cups or dish on a wire rack to cool. To serve, set the cups on serving plates or scoop from the baking dish into individual dishes. Dust with confectioners' sugar, then top with a dollop of whipped cream. ★

LEMON ZEST

If you bake or cook with lemons, limes, and oranges, chances are you'll frequently need citrus zest. Invest in a Microplane grater; Microplane evolved its range of graters from a traditional carpenter's rasp. Their graters allow you to effortlessly transform citrus peel into a fine, fluffy pile of zest.

pumpkin flan

serves 8

If pumpkin pie married caramel custard, their offspring would look like this pumpkin flan, which combines the best of both. It's a gorgeous and dramatic dessert that belies the ease with which it is made. Serve in the fall or winter when a special meal calls for an impressive ending that the guys will notice and appreciate.

½ cup granulated sugar

¾ cup light brown sugar

½ teaspoon ground cinnamon

½ teaspoon ground ginger

¼ teaspoon ground nutmeg

¼ teaspoon coarse salt

1 cup cooked pumpkin purée

1½ cups half-and-half or cream

5 large eggs, beaten

1 teaspoon pure vanilla extract

½ cup heavy cream, whipped

1 Preheat the oven to 350°F .

2 Put the granulated sugar in a 9-inch cake pan or pie plate, set on the center rack in the oven, and bake until the sugar is caramel colored, 8 to 12 minutes. Swirl to cover the bottom of the pie plate with the caramel.

3 In a large bowl, whisk together the brown sugar, cinnamon, ginger, nutmeg, and salt. Stir in the pumpkin purée. In a medium bowl, whisk together the half-and-half, eggs, and vanilla. Thoroughly blend the egg mixture into the pumpkin purée.

4 Set the pan in a large roasting pan and pour the custard over the caramel in the plate. Carefully pour enough hot tap water into the roasting pan to reach halfway up the sides of the pie plate. Bake until the custard is set, about 1 hour and 10 minutes. Cool and chill in the refrigerator. Run a knife around the outside edge of the flan and invert it onto a rimmed plate. Cut into wedges or scoop and serve with a dollop of whipped cream. ∗

Pumpkin Canned pumpkin, which is available all year round, works perfectly well in this recipe. But during the fall, when pumpkins are widely available, consider making homemade purée. Look for sugar pumpkins at the farmers' market. Or use your Halloween pumpkin after it's done its job.

Cut the pumpkin into pieces. Scrape out the seeds, place the pieces in a roasting pan, and cover with ¼ inch water. Cover with foil and cook at 375°F for 1 hour. Peel off the skin, remove any remaining seeds, and purée the flesh in a food processor or blender.

velvety chocolate pudding

makes 2 cups, or enough for 1 8-inch pie; serves 4 to 6

Chocolate mousse, molten chocolate cake, and flourless chocolate cake all deliver the same gooey chocolaty gratification that men—and women!—crave. But for home cooks with little time, few desserts supply the same ease and satisfaction as creamy chocolate pudding. Just spoon it into cups or bowls and serve. (This recipe is also a great basis for chocolate cream pie—make your favorite crust, spoon in the pudding, chill. Serve garnished with whipped cream and chocolate shavings.)

3½ tablespoons all-purpose flour

3 tablespoons best-quality cocoa powder

1 cup sugar

Hefty pinch of coarse salt

1½ cups milk

2 tablespoons unsalted butter, softened

1 large egg, well beaten

1 teaspoon pure vanilla extract

Whipped cream, for garnishing (optional)

1 In a medium bowl, whisk together the flour, cocoa powder, sugar, and salt. Press through a sieve into a medium saucepan to eliminate any lumps. Whisk in the milk.

2 Over medium heat, stir the mixture until thickened, about 2½ minutes. Be sure to get the spoon around the edges of the pan as the mixture thickens. Whisk if needed to combine well. Stir in the butter.

3 Whisk 1 tablespoon of the hot chocolate mixture into the beaten egg and return to the pudding in the pan. Stir in the vanilla and cook to completely thicken, 2 to 3 more minutes. Strain through a sieve and pour the pudding into four to six 6-ounce pudding cups. Serve warm, or cool first and chill until serving. Press plastic wrap directly on the surface of the pudding to prevent it from forming a skin (unless you like it!). Top with a dollop of whipped cream, if desired. ∗

rich rice pudding

serves 6 to 8

This dense creamy pudding brings solace and comfort to calorie counters who've fallen off the wagon. Whole milk, rice, sweet spices, and sugar combine for a perfect unctuous texture. Rum-soaked raisins make it a sophisticated dessert, but they can also be omitted. Serve with added whipped cream for those who can afford the extra calories. Otherwise, top with fresh or stewed fruit. Serve warm from the pot, or chilled. Either way, it's creamy and irresistible.

¼ cup currants or raisins (optional)

2 tablespoons golden rum (optional)

3 cups half-and-half or whole milk

½ cup rice, preferably jasmine or basmati

¼ cup sugar

½ teaspoon coarse salt

1 teaspoon pure vanilla extract

½ teaspoon ground cinnamon

¼ teaspoon ground nutmeg

1 If using the currants, soak them in the rum in a small bowl.

2 Place the half-and-half, rice, sugar, salt, vanilla, cinnamon, and nutmeg in a medium saucepan. Bring to a boil, stirring constantly. Reduce the heat to low and simmer for 20 minutes, continuing to stir.

3 Drain the currants and stir them into the pudding, then cook for an additional 2 minutes, or until the rice is al dente. Spoon the pudding into bowls and serve immediately, or spread it into a serving dish, cover, and chill. Press plastic wrap directly on the surface of the pudding to prevent it from forming a skin (unless you like it!). ✳

STEWED FRUIT TOPPING

When you have too much fruit, or it's become too soft for snacking, make a sweet sauce. Peel and cut fruit—such as apples, pears, peaches, or nectarines, or a mixture of all—into ½-inch pieces. Place in a small saucepan with ¼ cup water; 2 teaspoons of honey, pure maple syrup, or sugar; and a squeeze of lemon juice, if you like. Cover and simmer until soft. If you're using dried fruit, soak it in boiling water for 10 minutes, then drain and cook as directed.

crisp toffee chocolate bars

makes 16 bars

If you like a shortbread-type cookie, you'll like this "chocolate chip" version. It's caramel-flavored thanks to the brown sugar, buttery (here's where you might splurge on premium butter and chocolate), and has a great salty-sweet balance. And it's fast: pressing dough into a pan takes a lot less time and labor than individual dropped cookies. Plus, if your butter is soft enough, nothing more than a bowl and spoon are needed to make this. The trick is to cut the cookies into squares while they are still hot.

1 cup (2 sticks) unsalted butter, softened, plus more for the pan

1 cup light brown sugar

1 teaspoon coarse salt

1 teaspoon pure vanilla extract

2¼ cups sifted all-purpose flour

⅓ cup walnuts, chopped

1 cup semisweet chocolate chips

1 Preheat the oven to 350°F. Butter a 9 x 13-inch glass baking dish.

2 In a large bowl, beat together the butter, sugar, salt, and vanilla. Add the flour and mix well to combine. Stir in the walnuts and chocolate chips.

3 Press the dough into the prepared pan. Bake until golden and set, about 20 minutes. Cut into even squares while still warm. ∗

Chocolate

Dark, bittersweet, and semisweet chocolate can generally be interchanged in a recipe like this, as they all must contain at least 35 percent cacao. But the taste will be slightly different depending on whether you like a slightly bitter flavor or a sweeter one. I've opted for sweeter here.

oatmeal chocolate chip cookies

makes 24 cookies

Given the choice of only one cookie to eat, many of us would go for old-fashioned chocolate chip cookies. In this recipe, oatmeal adds texture *and* a healthy ingredient, which makes these cookies an excellent pick for a homemade boy cookie. The large, manly size makes them superb cold-milk dippers, too.

¾ cup all-purpose flour

½ teaspoon baking soda

¾ teaspoon coarse salt

8 tablespoons (1 stick) unsalted butter, softened, plus more for the pans

6 tablespoons granulated sugar

6 tablespoons light brown sugar

1 large egg

½ teaspoon pure vanilla extract

¼ teaspoon water

1 cup rolled oats

6 ounces semisweet chocolate chips

1 Preheat the oven to 375°F. Butter or line 2 rimmed baking sheets.

2 In a small bowl, whisk together the flour, baking soda, and salt.

3 In a large bowl, beat together the butter, sugars, egg, vanilla, and water. Add the flour mixture and stir to combine. Stir in the oats and chocolate chips.

4 Drop by teaspoonfuls onto the baking sheets, spacing the dough 1 inch apart. Bake for 10 to 12 minutes, until lightly golden in color. Remove to cooling racks. *

Cookie Baking Supplies If you bake a lot of cookies, or plan to start, invest in a few supplies that will make the effort much easier. Good-bye crusty pan, and hello:
● rimmed baking sheets (also known as jelly-roll pans or half-sheet pans) ● baking parchment paper or plastic heat-proof liners for baking sheets, to prevent cookies from sticking; Silpat is a good brand ● wire cooling racks to allow air to circulate and quickly cool cookies. Choose racks that fit inside your baking sheets so they can be used in a variety of ways. ● a thin metal spatula for lifting the baked cookies onto the cooling racks

---

For Successful Cookies
● Space the cookies at least 1 inch apart on the baking sheets to prevent them from melding together during baking. ● Rotate the baking sheets halfway through cooking to ensure even baking. ● Let the cookies cool on the hot baking sheets for one to two minutes before transferring to a wire rack.

chocolate drop cookies

makes 24 to 30 cookies

Another quick and simple drop cookie for a starting baker, this dough can be assembled, scooped onto cookie sheets, and frozen. Once the dough balls are frozen, stack them in a large resealable plastic bag in the freezer. When ready to bake them, place the frozen dough balls on a baking sheet and add an extra three to five minutes to the cooking time.

When my parents, brothers, and I used to arrive at my grandmother's home after an overnight car trip (packed in like sardines), Nonny had these cookies waiting for us, which were promptly inhaled. (Nonny's recipe calls for shortening, but I prefer to use butter.)

1½ cups all-purpose flour

¾ teaspoon baking powder

½ teaspoon coarse salt

1 cup (2 sticks) unsalted butter, softened, plus more for the pans

¾ cup sugar

1 large egg, lightly beaten

1 teaspoon pure vanilla extract

6 ounces bittersweet chocolate, melted

½ cup shredded coconut (optional)

⅓ cup milk

1 Preheat the oven to 350°F. Butter or line 2 rimmed baking sheets.

2 In a small bowl, whisk together the flour, baking powder, and salt.

3 In a large bowl, cream together the butter and sugar. Beat in the egg and vanilla. Blend in the melted chocolate and coconut, if desired. Alternately add the flour mixture and milk, ending with the flour. Drop dough by teaspoonfuls onto the baking sheets 1 inch apart. Bake for 10 to 15 minutes, until the edges are set and the centers are still soft. Remove to cooling racks. ∗

MELTING CHOCOLATE

On a Stove Top
Set a heat-proof bowl over simmering water. Add the chopped chocolate.
Stir constantly as it starts to melt.

In a Microwave
Place the chopped chocolate in a glass bowl. Microwave on medium for 1½ minutes.
Remove and stir. If the chocolate isn't melted, return it to the microwave and heat in increments of 30 seconds, stirring to avoid scorching, until fully melted.

no-bake
peanut butter–rice krispies cookies

makes 16 squares

Remember Rice Krispies Treats? Moms, grandmas, and aunts all over the country made them and barely got them out of the pan before kids inhaled them. These are amped up with peanut butter, making them even more addictive. For a young boy eager to work in the kitchen with you, this recipe is a good place to start. Yes, there's corn syrup, just this once.

1 cup light corn syrup

½ cup granulated sugar

½ cup light brown sugar

1½ cups salted peanut butter

2 teaspoons pure vanilla extract

4 cups Rice Krispies

1 Line a 9 x 13-inch baking pan with wax paper or baking parchment. Place the corn syrup and sugars in a large saucepan over medium heat and stir to combine. Bring to a boil. Remove from the heat.

2 Stir in the peanut butter and mix well to combine. Quickly stir in the vanilla and Rice Krispies. Spread into the lined baking pan. Cool and slice into squares. *

epilogue | the boys speak

"Mom, how on earth was the skin on the chicken always so crispy? Mom, what did you do to the banana chocolate-chip cookies that made them so fricken delicious? The answers to these questions and my attempts to replicate the good vibes of my childhood at your table transport me back to the family kitchen."

—Calder (eldest son)

"One might wonder what people mean when they say put some love into the food, but one thing is for sure, my mother never has a shortage of love in her food, and I think that is why she has kept all three of her boys mad hungry for her food."

—Miles (middle son)

"When I was little, I never realized how lucky I was to eat my parents' amazing food day in and day out. Now that I am older and more aware of the quality and love put into these meals, I savor every bite and hope one day I can cook for my family and let them experience the same joy."

—Luca (youngest son)

acknowledgments

Thank-you to all my favorite man cooks—husbands, sons, brothers, fathers, and friends who've inspired this book— especially C. George, Jim, David and Peter Scala, and the Quinn males who are my gifts that just keep on giving.

Photographer Mikkel Vang's vision led our shoot team of Michelle Wong, Jennifer Aaronson, and Calder Quinn— with too much fun while working! James Dunlinson's outsized creativity influenced this book from the beginning to the end of its making.

Trust and patience from Ann Bramson, Sigi Nacson, Jan Derevjanik, and the Artisan team is much appreciated. Also, to Jennifer S. Muller, of Lucky Tangerine, who created this innovative book design.

Carla Glasser, my agent, is a faithful compass and friend.

Lasting gratitude to the many chefs, cooks, purveyors, and colleagues over the years from whom I continue to learn every day, most notably Martha Stewart.

index